Love That Works

A Guide to Enduring Intimacy

Wendy Strgar

Printed in the United States of America

For information, contact
Love Words Press
1891 Lincoln Street
Eugene, Oregon 97401

Strgar, Wendy
Love That Works: A Guide to Enduring Intimacy/ Wendy Strgar — 1st ed.

ISBN 978-1-4507-3428-8
Love Words Press books are available for special promotions,
premiums, or corporate training.
For information, contact info@lovewordspress.com

First edition

Editor: Zanne Miller
Cover design: Jan Ryan
Book typography: Jan Ryan
Cover photo: Fotosearch
Back cover photo: Andrea Allen Sis

LOVE
WORDS
PRESS

PRAISE FOR LOVE THAT WORKS

"In Love That Works, Wendy Strgar has given us a road map to more satisfying, sustainable relationships. This is an excellent book that anyone who is partnered or married should own. Love That Works is one of the best books I've read about the hard but rewarding work of what it means to love." —Debby Herbenick, Ph.D., author of Because It Feels Good: A Woman's Guide to Sexual Pleasure & Satisfaction

"I love this book! It reads like the 'Zen of relationships'— powerful quotes, followed up with a combination of memoir, case studies and philosophy. Wendy has obviously learned a lot from her own marriage and those of others, and she shares her insights in a powerful and memorable way. She has organized her thoughts with metaphors of the four elements: earth, air, fire and water— as the basic ingredients of a lasting marriage. It's a very helpful book, and obviously a labor of love." —Tina B. Tessina, Ph.D., (aka "Dr. Romance") psychotherapist and author of Money, Sex and Kids: Stop Fighting About the Three Things That Can Ruin Your Marriage

"Love That Works is the playbook of love. Love is a complicated sport and Coach Strgar lays out the x's and o's to help you succeed! It is a practical, every day guide to understanding and managing your love life. Enter the "laboratory of love" and you'll get to stand back and see what real people do to sustain their loving relationships. Keep it handy, because when things get difficult, you'll want to refer to Love That Works."
—Mark Schoen, Ph.D. Founder, SexSmartFilms.com

"*Love That Works* is an honest, loving, heartfelt cure for our culture of relationship cynicism. In discussing her own marriage and the relationships of others, we are confronted with hope, forgiveness, and vulnerability, through examples that both empower and give us courage in opening ourselves to love. A gem of a book for those seeking greater depth and meaning in their relationships. This book can help any love be sustainable!" —P. Michele Sugg, MSW, LCSW AASECT Certified Sex Therapist; Sex Therapy Advisor, Alexander Foundation for Women's Health

"Wendy offers a medicine that's sorely needed in this time of conflict, difficulty and stress, and she prescribes it honestly, delicately and with the utmost respect. Hers is a great and important medicine for our time." —Nina Simons, Founder of Bioneers

"Love and work are the cornerstones of our humanness."
— Sigmund Freud

For Franc
and his enduring love.

Dedicated to my children,
Ana, Ian, Luke and Emma.

For all the ways I have learned to love you—
and all the ways that I hope love will envelop you.

ACKNOWLEDGMENTS

This book would not be in your hands were it not for the skilled and loving attention of two incredible editors who I am proud to also call friends. The book would not have happened without either of them. Michelle Theriault, a remarkably skilled writer/journalist herself, shaped the book's direction and structure. Our long conversations about the meaning of love and relationships clarified for both of us why the book needed to get done. I still miss our "power meetings" and hearing her recount the wonders of the world that she is continuously encountering. The first copy of the book is hers for her wedding.

Zanne Miller, an incredible writer and experienced editor, took over the stewardship of the book and has demonstrated a remarkable capacity to refine the meanings and depth of my own writing as well as a strong clear vision of the book's final form. Her confidence was infectious, and the pleasure she had in applying her skills to the many steps of book production made the process rewarding.

My daughter Ana, soon graduating with a journalism degree, blesses me with her understanding of grammar and punctuation every night. Her attention to detail was helpful in finishing this book. She is the sounding board for my deepest ideas and has taught me always about what pure kindness looks like.

Thanks also goes to our designer Jan Ryan, who helped find the right clothes for these thoughts, so we all came out looking stylish and contemporary.

Many other people figure into the stories that make up the pages of the book. These couples made me the loveologist I am today. I am grateful for the confidence they showed in me as well as the courage they demonstrated in sharing their stories of trying to love over and over again. A word of thanks should also be directed at the business, Good Clean Love, which started in my kitchen and has grown into a product company that I am proud to say I founded. Our customers have often become our friends, and knowing them inspired this book.

My own family life has long served as a living laboratory of love, and I thank my husband, Franc and my four children, Ana, Ian, Luke and Emma for all they have taught me about the resilience and strength that comes from love that lasts. The best decision I ever made and one that has made the rest of my life possible was marrying Franc, and I am grateful every day, even the really difficult ones, for his devotion and constancy.

Each of my children is a lightning rod for my heart in a different way. Watching them become themselves and sharing their lives with so much depth and intimacy has been the healing journey of my life.

I have always felt fortunate to be able to do work that most deeply reflects who I am and what I believe I was put here to do. For this great privilege, I am indebted to all of my friends and family who have encouraged me to speak from my heart and who were gracious enough to listen. I am convinced that the only real purpose for our lives is to manifest love that works and reaches out in ever increasing concentric circles. How blessed I am to have a life dedicated to that cause.

P R E F A C E

There is not another country or culture in the world that craves long-term relationships yet fails at them at such a pace as the United States. By expecting our relationships to make us happy and meet our needs instead of recognizing their capacity to teach us how to love more, we refuse the daily, messy work of relating—learning how to communicate, negotiate and master shared difficulties and challenges.

This misunderstanding impacts our ability to commit as well. True happiness comes as a result of the sustained emotional investment in other people. Commitment comes from developing the ability to remember that you really love someone, even if you aren't feeling it.

That said, it is easy to get completely mired in facing the many challenges of building a life together, and forget that relationships are also built on shared experiences of pleasure and fun. By injecting playful intimacy and novel problem-solving experiences you actually strengthen the bond that allows you to deal with the challenges that life inevitably generates.

Ultimately our loving relationships are the most gentle and effective education we engage in to become the person we want to be. Rather than focusing on finding the right partner, commitment works best when we approach it as a method of personal growth.

The cultural myth of the perfect partner or soul mate is a distraction that keeps us from the real work of love. This book is dedicated to helping you in that work and in creating love that lasts.

CONTENTS

CHAPTER 1

Love That Works

Making Your Love Sustainable

We all want to be loved. Yet in a world driven by commercial messages about entitled happiness and freedom of choice, our relationships bear the burden of the misguided belief, that, like the stuff we accumulate, they are interchangeable and disposable if they do not meet our needs. Instead of recognizing another's capacity to teach us how to love more, we refuse the daily, messy work of relating—learning how to communicate, negotiate and master shared difficulties and challenges.

This misunderstanding impacts our ability to commit as well. True happiness comes as a result of sustained emotional investment in other people. When we commit, we agree to not measure our relationship on a daily barometer: Although there may be many a day when honoring our commitment to our relationships contradicts our momentary feelings of frustration and disappointment, commitment comes from developing the ability to remember that you really love someone, even if you aren't feeling it.

Ultimately our loving relationships are the most gentle and effective education we engage in to become the person we want to be. Rather than focusing on finding the right partner, commitment works best when we approach it as a method of personal growth.

The late psychologist Caryl Rusbult coined the notion of the "Michelangelo effect" in describing how committed, loving relationships have the power to sculpt us into the people we want to be.[1] Michelangelo used to say that the figures he created were asleep within the stones, waiting to be discovered. Love that works, over time, can do this for us: We both reflect and elicit the values that we commit to creating with our partners.

I am in the business of love.

As the work of love changes you and helps you grow into the person you want to be, the relationship creates a commitment of its own. The work becomes its own incentive, as both parties involved recognize that their individual well-being is linked to that of their partner and their relationship.

The cultural myth of the perfect partner or soul mate is a distraction that keeps us from the real work of love. This book is dedicated to finding the many ways that love will sculpt you and your life—the real one that exists now— into a work of art—one that is worthy of you and the one you love.

I am in the business of love. For the last seven years, I have been building the business and the idea of Good Clean Love. In manufacturing and selling our own formulations of organic personal lubricants and all-natural aphrodisiac love products, I found my real passion. I am a teacher, and what I most passionately and convincingly communicate about has become our tag line: Making Love Sustainable. I do much of this teaching through my blog at www.goodcleanlove.com.

The thousands of you that have sought me out, written to me and continuously opened your hearts and relationships to me have dubbed me a "loveologist." It is a both an honor and responsibility that I feel lucky to give my life to.

The stories, inspirations, and lessons I share here are hard won like yours. The original impetus for Good Clean Love came from a search for healthy and clean products that didn't make me sick after intimacy. The pursuit of making sense of love in my own life is the inspiration for this book.

We all live in a laboratory of love—if we are awake. Every day, there are opportunities to learn to love the people who inhabit your world. Some days it comes out looking just like you planned. Other days, the relationship is so far off that it is barely recognizable. Most days, we all live somewhere in between, striving to see the best in others and to act from the best in ourselves.

It is no different for me; I have been married to the same man for more than 25 years. Together we have four kids, all of them hovering at some stage of adolescence. When I was their age, my parents had a messy, violent divorce, which at the time forced me to recognize the big gap between the kids I knew who had families at their back and kids like me, who were on their own. From this experience, creating family and learning what it meant to keep promises became the driving force in my life.

This has not been an easy path. But if you believe the maxim that "you only fail when you quit," then you can always agree to keep it going one more day. Every relationship is really something that you agree to one day at a time. Anyone can learn to make their love sustainable. The skill set to love over time exists as a seed in all of us. But without careful tending and cultivation, it will not thrive. Sustainable love is not driven by the sexy early feelings of falling in love. It thrives by building skills in communication, keeping your promises, controlling your thoughts instead of being controlled by them, and being a curious and willing lover.

This combination of behaviors—what I call the Ecology of Love— is what I teach and write about every week in my sustainable love letters. The Ecology of Love is the natural habitat where love can grow and nourish the relationship and the world. The understanding of it came to me slowly, but the more I study and teach it, the more that this natural ecosystem of love makes sense.

I hope it can help you to understand your own relationship in a way that renews your commitment and allows you the freedom to fall in love again and again.

Most days I feel unbelievably blessed and grateful to say that I am more in love with my husband than ever before. I am not in a fairy-tale-happily-ever-after marriage, however. I don't think those exist, except for maybe a moment at a time. But I am devoted to exploring what there is to stay for.

The concept of sustainability can be applied to our primary relationships, which at their best are the most natural system of regeneration that we have. Cultivating the skills that help us love even through the most difficult moments is both the gift and the challenge of building a family.

As we begin to appreciate that being in relationship and having a family and history with someone is a precious resource, we can begin to focus on the parts of our relating skill set that may need attention. The huge amounts of trust, time and loving intention that we invest early in our relationships are actually renewable resources and the currency of our future health and well-being. Sustaining your love when relationships are challenging—through healthy thinking and loving words and actions—not only keeps your own intimacy vibrant, but becomes a living legacy for future generations.

Creating an Ecology of Love

Our planet's atmosphere, our invisible ozone layer, is intrinsic to the health of everything that lives on our planet. It is so thin that it is transparent. It is only now, when confronted with its fragility, that we realize how critical it is to our survival. This fragility of our atmospheric conditions provides a sound metaphor for how the language of environmental sustainability translates to the concept of Making Love Sustainable. Real love, the kind that endures after the "falling in love" goes away, is the atmosphere that contains our relationships and allows families to flourish. Just like the earth's atmosphere, it is as fragile as it is powerful and only recognizably so when it is compromised. Learning to care for it is a task we must embrace for our survival.

The atmosphere in which love can thrive can be defined. The elements that build a healthy and sustainable container of love are not complex. They are all skill-based, which means that with attention and education, anyone can improve upon them. These elements work together and depend on each other to create emotionally intelligent intimate relationships.

Try This:

What the heck, self-disclose a little bit more. Sharing intimate feelings and thoughts about your life is literally a breath of fresh air, even when doing so is challenging or difficult to share. Be your authentic self, and allow your partner the grace to do the same.

The Four Elements

The ground of our relationships rests in our thoughts. This is the foundation of your relationship.

Our thoughts are incredibly powerful: They can keep us connected or they can drive us apart. When was the last time you monitored the emotional quality of your thinking about your partner? Giving people the benefit of the doubt, giving up the need to be right, and looking for what is lovable in your partner will help you to choose thoughts that sustain a loving atmosphere.

The water of our relationships happens in the ebb and tide of togetherness. This is how we show up for each other and keep our promises.

Showing up for someone isn't about creating quality time and special date nights, although every now and again it is nice to take that time and really be together. Adding safety to your relationship has more to do with making different choices about the little things. For example, instead of reading the paper after work, offer to help with dinner. Sharing the annoying details of a life together speaks volumes about your priorities. "Your needs matter to me" is one of the most important messages you can send.

The air of relationships flows with our ability to communicate. What we say and whether we feel heard is the basic currency that enriches or bankrupts our relationships.

Communication happens with both words and actions. Not being able to self-disclose or share important life events literally takes the air out of relationships. The goal of communicating should be connection; sometimes that might mean engaging in conversation that isn't particularly interesting to you, or learning to listen more attentively. Or it might not be about the words; it might be how you pay attention sitting side by side. Begin your work in this area with sensitivity, and don't take missteps personally. Men and women have very different ways of expressing and listening to each other, but that doesn't mean they can't learn to communicate well.

The fire of relationships is ignited through physical touch. Cultivating a passionate, tender and safe place to explore sexuality with the one we love is the height of intimacy.

Many people believe that if the physical intimacy in their relationship were stronger, the rest would simply improve. Usually the reverse is true. A great sexual relationship and ongoing passion is the result of how you think, communicate and show up for the people you love. Not the reverse. Intimate lives that are fueled in all of these areas tend to be the ones where people can truly open up, discover their own passion, and be generous with their sexuality.

So consider each of these aspects of your relationship—thinking, talking, showing up and physical intimacy—and ask yourself where you could improve. Where would you like to see more from your partner? By paying attention to each of the four elements, you can work to make the relationship more open, more secure and more accepting, as well as more passionate.

This book is organized around these four elements of sustainable love. You can read it any way you like: front to back, or just by opening to any section. Hopefully you will find what you are looking for. Creating a safe and loving relationship isn't difficult— it's about the small choices we all make every day. With that in mind, here's to making love sustainable.

CHAPTER 2

Laying the Groundwork

The quality of your thoughts, especially concerning the people you love, creates the ground that allows for the growth in all of your relationships. Many people are unaware of the effects of their own thoughts or the powerfully destructive effect that negative thinking has on our relationships. Whether from unexamined ideas from our family of origin or unhealthy influences in popular culture, negative thinking and its projections limit the possibility of fully experiencing love in our relationships.

Some of the most common bad thinking that I witness over and over when people share their romance stories with me is the idea that the relationship that you are in should be easy, easier, less work, less demanding…and that being in relationship with your mate should make you happy, satisfied, or content.

I remember vividly the afternoons I spent sitting at the park with a friend, watching our kids play. Our favorite topic was our respective husbands. I looked forward to sharing my husband's most recent offense: It felt good to have someone else really understand the frustration that I couldn't communicate to him about his fathering style, or the lack of it, as I saw it at the time. The conversations only fueled my self-righteous, negative thoughts about him, and I would arrive home angry and bitter about my partnership.

I didn't realize the power these thoughts had in my relationship until a relatively new acquaintance joined the conversation at the park one windy day in the fall. Hearing my rant, she asked point blank: "If it's so bad, why are you staying with him?"

I couldn't respond at the moment, but after weeks of soul searching, I realized that my negative spin wasn't necessarily "the Truth." As I began to experiment with seeing the positive in my husband's actions, he reciprocated.

The change was remarkable: As we began to accept each other as we really were, I could see again what I liked about him. We realized quickly that most of our arguments were variations on the same theme: "Why won't you be the way I want you to be?" We learned that it is impossible to love who someone is if you are always waiting for them to become your definition of "lovable."

The work of changing your thoughts begins with learning to actually witness them. Try it for a week. Don't judge yourself when you see bad thinking patterns, but be willing to acknowledge how your thinking is affecting your mood, your communication, and your ability to commit to the people you love. With practice, you can catch these mind habits earlier and earlier and develop an awareness that allows you the freedom to choose how you want to think.

Try to approach your relationship with this in mind: This relationship is not here to make me happy (satisfied, content, or fill in the blank). It is here to teach me to love.

Holding loving thoughts of your partner is one of the most powerful change agents available to building sustainable love. The energy of love that envelops both partners creates a safety net of unconditional support. This, in turn allows the family to grow and change as the individual members enjoy the freedom of discovering themselves.

You Get What You Need

Junie and Michael first bonded over the mutual position that the Rolling Stones were, in fact, superior to the Beatles. At first Michael seemed like everything Junie didn't quite want: He wasn't classically handsome or athletic, he was a little awkward around most people—and besides, she was hung up on another guy altogether. But she'd let him in, as a friend, and had found herself feeling warm, happy, and secure in his presence—feeling very much like herself in a way she never had before.

She was still fixated on this unattainable other man, he of the guitar solos and the moody brown eyes, who planned to ride his motorcycle around India after graduation. (Michael planned to do something sensible like become an actuary and an accountant.) Junie chased her crush for years, following him to India, where she spent several months sick with food poisoning on the back of a Triumph motorbike. She came back to the United States still in love with him. He'd return—she was sure of it.

Meanwhile, she reconnected with Michael, who lived in a cozy little apartment with a great record collection. They would make dinner together and laugh for hours, listening to "Exile on Main Street." They didn't talk much about her love in India; her feelings for her crush faded as her friendship with Michael grew. It was a love that crept around Junie's heart like kudzu.

A wedding, fifteen years, and two children later, she remembers the brown-eyed guitar god, the adventurer she had been so sure she was meant to be with. And she knows that life has a way of giving you what is right, even when you don't know it.

"You can't always get what you want, but if you try sometimes, you just might find, you get what you need…."

That Rolling Stones refrain is playing repeatedly in my head of late. This is as true a love song as I have ever known. Although I would never have thought it in my earlier years, what I know of love that has staying power is that it is rarely about what you want. Cultivating sustainable love is mostly about growing up a bit. It's about learning how to accept what you get, turning it into what you want, or at least embracing it as what you need.

I experienced this at work the other day, when a customer called to reorder some products. An articulate and educated cancer survivor, she told me things about my own products that I never knew. When I asked her if she received my newsletters, she said yes, but that there wasn't much there for her. She had done this work already. I like to believe that my messages make a difference for everyone, but the truth is that people take what they need, and it might not be what is most important for you.

"You can't always get what you want..."

The song also echoes my struggles to find peace in my relationship with my father. A difficult personality, a pain-filled childhood, and years of resentment and hatred converge at our every meeting. In the past, these feelings were my reaction to not getting the compassionate witnessing and loving attention that we all crave. Lately the pain is about bearing witness to my own struggle to transform my inner relationship to my past and to him. But negative feelings like hatred and resentment rarely impact the object of our feelings. Instead, they keep us stuck in the same habitual patterns that we have come to associate with the relationship. In the case of my father, I will never get what I want from that relationship, but I am starting to know how to look for what I need.

"You Can't Always Get What You Want" has been a love song in my marriage for decades. Learning how to see the relationship that we have as the one we need instead of lamenting its shortcomings (when compared to what we thought we wanted) is a lifelong effort. It is easy to be confused and to want to refuse the love that a partner can give, if it doesn't look or feel the way that we think it should. This happens most frequently in my marriage when I am deep in battles with my own demons.

That's why it's important to look within: When we are most lost to ourselves and unable to accept our weaknesses or recognize our strengths, all of the places where our closest relationships fall short become unbearable. It is too painful to recognize the moments when we are incapable of loving. Blaming the other is a ready survival mechanism. Often the response is so habitual that we don't even have the time to choose a different response. "But if you try sometimes, you just might find, you get what you need." It is definitely worth trying.

Waiting for the Spring

In the seasons of their marriage, this was a particularly long and bleak winter. Joy was in the midst of writing her dissertation, and her husband, Paul, was similarly occupied with a research grant that could lead to a breakthrough in his career as a biologist. They had been a couple that slid smoothly into marriage—one summer day, after they had been together about two years, they had been swimming in an Oregon river, and Paul had casually asked if she thought they should get married. They did, the next day, at the courthouse.

But the easiness and warmth of their lives in graduate school didn't move with them to a big new city with big new responsibilities, the least of which seemed to be marriage. Joy was so used to having fun and being happy with Paul; this new distance between them made her feel like a stranger. She started to think that maybe this relationship wasn't worth it after all—or maybe they'd rushed into marriage. It just didn't seem possible that a relationship could feel this cold and bleak for such a long time.

Just as she was about to give up, she saw small signs of hope. Paul was less preoccupied with the goings-on in his lab. She turned in a first draft of her dissertation. The pressure on them abated, and they began to laugh together again. She felt relieved that a thawing was possible, and wondered how many other people walked away at the height of winter, without ever seeing spring around the corner.

The goal of making a relationship sustainable should not just be to stay, but rather, to find and cultivate the places in the relationship that are worth staying for, to re-imagine your commitment to a healthy curiosity about the mystery of the other person, and to allow for the ebb and flow of intimacy that is a normal part of loving relationships.

The other day I ran into an old friend while dropping off my son for basketball practice. The last time I saw her, she was celebrating her first anniversary with her second husband. After a tragic ending to her first marriage, she seemed radiant—they both did. That was a year ago. Her boys were in transition but welcomed having a father again. Now, she is in the final stages of her second divorce. She said it was a difficult transition for him: He became unhappy shortly after they were married. Marriage and their ready-made family had taken a toll on his music career, and they both decided rather quickly it would be easier to split. I expressed my sorrow for her, but she replied, almost cheerfully, that she was fine—better actually than when they were struggling to make it work.

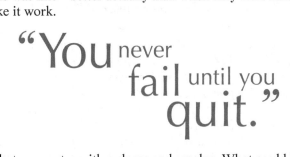

"You never fail until you quit."

I left that encounter with sadness and resolve. What could I learn from all the leaving that I see going on around me? When should relationships be ended? What amount of time and work constitutes "enough?" These are the questions that encircle many of my conversations with friends in various stages of leaving their relationships.

Two things come to mind when I talk to my friends about these endings. First, there's a quote I have hanging on my office wall: "You never fail until you quit." This idea has become a primary premise in maintaining all of my relationships. If communication is the currency of relationship, then walking away from the communication is certainly its death.

Sustainable love, and not only romantic love, requires acknowledging and accepting all of the "seasons" of a relationship as they come to you. It isn't reasonable to walk away from the winters in love—not the snuggly-by-the-fire winter, but the cold, bleak emptiness and other feelings that have you wondering how you ever could have said yes to this. It's unreasonable to think that a newly sprouted seed can sustain a cold frost without some assistance. Sustaining love is about learning to wait for the spring, trusting that it will come, and creating the warmth that will help the thaw to begin.

Simply put, creating sustainable love requires a decision to give up the fantasy that relationships exist to make us happy. They have moments of deep and profound joy, like a jump in the lake on a hot summer day. But that is not what they are there for. They exist to teach us to love.

The Real Work

Susan was diagnosed with breast cancer a week before her 37th birthday. It seemed young still, to her—she felt young when she was out on the boat sailing, she felt young when she was standing in front of her fifth-grade classroom. The media are saturated with stories about breast cancer survivors, but when the doctor gave her the diagnosis, it still seemed like a scene from a bad movie about somebody else's life.

In the moments after the diagnosis, the doctor left her in a small room that smelled of disinfectant. She stared at the posters of internal organs and proper hand washing techniques. She felt as if she was suddenly in a land with no map, no atlas—it was uncharted. Her life as she had envisioned it seemed to be over.

Nothing was as she'd imagined it. At home, she found herself comforting her distraught husband, not the other way around. She'd always seen him as the strong, constant force. Now he seemed to be falling to pieces imagining life without her. The doctor had given her a fifty percent chance of recovery: She was young, but the cancer was fairly advanced.

All of the problems with her marriage that had incubated over the past decade seemed to rise to the surface. If she survived this cancer, she decided, things had to be different. In the end, her husband rallied, and she realized that the way he seemed to fall apart signified just how much he loved her.

Through days and weeks of chemotherapy, radiation, nausea, and hair loss, she stepped away from her busy life and watched as every bit of routine fell away, leaving a painful, brilliant truth. She would recover, but things needed to change in her relationship. The best way that she could heal herself for now was to love.

It may be that when we no longer know what to do—we have
come to our real work—and that when we no longer
know which way to go, we have come to our real journey.

The mind that is not baffled is not employed.

The impeded stream is the one that sings.

— Wendell Berry, *Remembering: A Novel.*

More often than we would like to admit, and often accompanying
a significant loss, we confront the brutal truth that we really
don't know where we are going or what to do. It is a disquieting
realization. A moment of not knowing will show us more about
ourselves than all of the days we spend feeling certain of the
next step.

Living with ourselves during these groundless moments of pure
bafflement is not easy. All of our critical inner voices seem to
shout louder, and small inconveniences have the weight of real
problems. Stepping out of our stories to gain a truer perspective
feels like a steep climb up. When things feel hard is when I cut
myself while chopping vegetables or stub my toe on a couch
that hasn't moved in years. I seem to attract impediments like a
magnet. Keeping the mind focused on routine chores requires
effort. It is especially hard to maintain the caretaking of others
when we feel lost to ourselves.

So it is not surprising, but it hits like a double whammy, when
our relationship falters under the strain of holding ourselves on
the edge of the unknown. A difficult time is a lonely time, and
often requires a language of emotions that is as unfamiliar as the
experience itself.

Distancing ourselves from our loved ones during these times
does not help, but it is easy to do, and all the more so when our
bafflement comes from the relationship itself. Relationships go
through these same places of groundlessness and, precisely when
we need to lean in and learn how to love more, we pull away.

"Goodness suffices and endures forever; on this throughout its years true love depends." In 43 B.C., Ovid wrote these words, perhaps as a solution to the feelings of up-against-the-wall, no-place-to-turn kind of groundlessness that humans have faced since the beginning of time.

"Goodness suffices and endures forever..."

So, when things are difficult: Be kind to yourself and practice goodness with everyone you love, or better still everyone you encounter. Watch for goodness around you and feel happy that you were there to bear witness. It sounds simple, but it isn't. It requires vigilance and practice and a willingness to let go of the habitual thoughts that trap us.

Fear is often the emotion that holds us tightly in our moments of loss, and it has been said that love is the antidote to fear. So try to love more when you are lost, beginning with yourself. I recently read that altruistic behavior actually heals.[2] We feel better when we help other people, because in the act of offering love, we gain the perspective to find our way back to a path with heart.

The Five Percent Rule

Jake and Nicole had arrived in a place in their marriage that felt endless, with drifting doldrums and a bleak outlook. Both were busy making partner at their respective law firms, and raising a child in the midst of it left little time for each other.

Nicole knew what could happen if they let their wake-work-kids-sleep routine sink roots into their lives. They had seen too many of their friends divorce after a few years like this. They'd end up strangers who lived together, and their son would eventually end up alternating weekends between his parents' houses. She confronted Jake about the growing distance between them, and to her surprise he seemed concerned as well. They agreed to try a little harder each day to bridge the gap between their schedules and their lives.

But even as she'd made the commitment, she felt herself tiring: It took so much effort to simply perform the basic functions of her life, much less spend extra energy on something that wasn't even broken, at least officially. They'd said yes to the project, and Jake had retreated to the TV room, Nicole to the bedroom. As usual.

But the next day, Jake called to ask how her day was going, and they met for lunch. Though they worked just blocks from each other, Nicole usually ate a sandwich at her desk as she plowed through more work. It was a quick lunch, but they shared a conversation about something other than the dishwasher and the yard—and a kiss on the cheek on their way out the door.

Nicole walked back to her office building. She couldn't believe what a difference one lunch made. They promised each other that even if they couldn't make time for anything else, they'd do that. She knew she couldn't change everything, but just this one small effort was already feeling like it could change something. It would be their extra five percent.

Someone told me a long time ago that if you can change any area of your life by a consistent five percent, the effects will be remarkable. The truth of this is mirrored in the reality of global warming. Even changes of a single degree can change everything. Just a few years ago what was imperceptible even to scientists was altering the landscape of our collective future. This five percent rule applies to our personal ecosystems as well. The smallest of changes in how we communicate in, show up for, and think about our relationship can and do alter its course.

Bad things happen fast, good things take time: This is the caveat about how the five percent rule works. Relationships are fragile ecosystems; just as in the aftermath of a storm, rebuilding and recuperation is a process that takes the time and patience that is the daily work of sustaining.

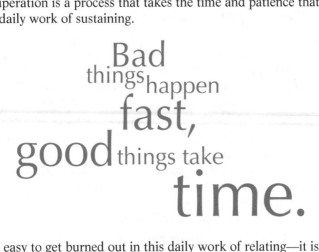

Bad things happen fast, good things take time.

It is easy to get burned out in this daily work of relating—it is the hardest work that we are asked to do. Life can be busy and complicated, and people can be annoying, even the very best of them—especially when you live with them and are charged with their care. This fact can apply to growing families or aging parents as easily as it does to our primary partner. Keeping relationships healthy and being willing to heal the ones that are ailing requires a resolution to keep the five percent rule in action. It is being willing to perform the one extra act of kindness each day. It is calling your partner for lunch and asking about his or her day, and taking the time to listen even when you feel you have heard enough. It is finding the energy to be intimate even when you don't feel connected. It is the laundry, and the dishes, and one more trip to the grocery store.

The five percent rule is a good resolution to make no matter what your life situation. Another way of thinking about it is as a continuous improvement plan, where we agree to remain attentive to our own attitude and willingness to participate. It acknowledges that we aren't going to be perfect or expect perfection, but rather with realistic intentions, we can strive to be just a bit better than yesterday. It is not impatient but respects the time that it takes for small, seemingly imperceptible changes to be felt and experienced.

Making a resolution to live with a five percent improvement plan is a heroic act. Not only do you courageously surrender to the unpredictable yet inevitable falling apart that happens in every life, but you simultaneously hold your heart open to trying to make the small acts of living softer and more bearable for the people you love. It is a resolution that you can keep, because it commits you to a process rather than an outcome—and gives you the freedom to miss the mark some days.

So go ahead, resolve to get better at whatever you choose—or what the heck, resolve to get better in your whole life. But start with five percent. It's plenty.

No Going Back

Adele was strangely jealous of some of her divorced friends. After decades of marriage, some had parted ways with their husbands— after an accumulation of unmet expectations, festering emotional wounds, an occasional affair that could be neatly summarized on paper as "irreconcilable differences." Some had embarked on their new singledom by taking yoga classes, going back to school or traveling to places such as India and Costa Rica.

For a few, new love had come into their lives. This was not the love that she and her husband knew: Sitting at a kitchen table at midnight waiting for a rebellious teenager to come home, re-mortgaging the house to help pay for the fancy liberal arts school that had accepted their daughter. That love wore old, ugly slippers and a ratty bathrobe and cleaned leaves out of the gutters on Sundays. This new, divorcée love involved expensive wine and boating. One friend always described these dates, shining with newness, as "ridiculously fun."

When was the last time Adele and Pete had done something "ridiculously fun?" Adele began to tally the disappointments and losses in her 25-year-old marriage. It was as if she was standing over an ugly, gaping hole and staring into what could have been—trivial stuff, like trips not taken, and less trivial stuff, like career paths deferred. These divorced friends seemed to be getting a second chance, a new start. The accumulation of life—painful and not—had a weighing, deadening effect on her relationship. Her divorced friends had found the courage to let go of their past relationships, and some for good reasons. But the opposite was true, too: You had to know when to stand over the past and bless it.

No, no, there is no going back.

Less and less you are that possibility you were.

More and more you have become those lives and deaths that have belonged to you.

You have become a sort of grave containing much that was and is no more in time, beloved then, now and always.

And so you have become a sort of tree standing over a grave.

Now more than ever you can be generous toward each day that comes, young, to disappear forever and yet remain unaging in the mind.

Every day you have less reason not to give yourself away.

— Wendell Berry, "A Timbered Choir."

There is a great relief to accepting where you are in life. When we let go of all the might haves or should haves or could haves and see what is left, real life begins. The idea that hindsight is 20/20 vision doesn't really respect the fact that when that moment was fully present, you did the best you could. You made the best decision that was available at the time; you loved as much as you were able to. Giving up this looking back is the way to step into the days that you have.

This wisdom of "No Going Back" is useful in learning to embrace our current relationships as well as our relationship history. Bearing witness to the grave of our past loves, the lessons learned, the promises kept and broken, the path that led you to where you stand today, gives you the freedom to be open to this moment.

My parents have been divorced for twice as many years as they were married, yet the stories of the pain and suffering they inflicted on each other remain as fresh in their minds as the days they were happening. By contrast, a new friend recently divorced after her husband left her for his secretary—not long after she gave birth to their third child—bears no ill will. "We are friends," she says. She doesn't share the story of blame with her kids. She didn't give up her belief in her ability to love. She cried for her loss, but she didn't throw herself in the grave.

Holding on to what should have or might have been in your relationship can be destructive. You cannot go forward from the past, only from the present. Finding the courage to let go is the primary act of loving.

You cannot go forward from the past, only from the present.

Love and Happiness

Kristine had always felt like an impediment to her parents' happiness, not a source of it. She'd been raised in a household where the clinking of ice into a highball glass was shorthand for emotional expression. Her parents were silent, depressed alcoholics who hated each other and would have divorced if such a thing were acceptable, but who maintained a flat impression of suburban tranquility for appearances' sake.

Kristine was a product of this marriage, and felt badly about it. Her parents seemed to tolerate her, but as an adult she did not have a single memory of an expression of love. Life and relationships were about enduring and pretending. Kristine hoped that she'd someday meet a man who loved her, but she couldn't see why someone would.

It was no surprise, then, that the men she picked early in life treated her much like her father had treated her mother: as if they were doing her a favor by spending time with her, and as if she had to scramble for their continued affections. It led to an ugly series of romances, if you could call them that, where Kristine gave and gave and gave (sex, rent money, a shoulder to cry on, more second chances than she should have) and got nothing in return.

After yet another long bout of crying over her misfortune, Kristine looked at herself in a restroom mirror one day and saw something different. Instead of an ugly, lonely little girl she saw a woman with a good heart—a woman who deserved something better than the parental hand she'd been dealt.

> The supreme happiness in life is the conviction that we are loved—loved for ourselves or rather, loved in spite of ourselves.
> —Victor Hugo

Serious scientific inquiry has proven this quote to be true.[3] By all measures of health and well-being, the single most significant predictor of lifetime happiness and longevity is involvement in an intimate and loving relationship.[4]

Yet even with all this evidence of the power of loving bonds, we are caught in a culture that throws away relationships as though they were empty soda cans.

Why is that? Are some people just lucky in love? Some of it may be luck. If you grew up as a wanted and beloved child of happy parents, chances are good that a positive and secure romantic style is on your side. If you didn't have these advantages, then chances are you fall into the avoidant or anxious romantic styles. All of these profiles or personality traits are linked to a child's ability to attach early in life. New research suggests that these early childhood patterns go a long way in explaining people's lifelong struggles with relationships.[5]

As the names suggest, avoidant and anxious romantic profiles can make it difficult for people to learn the very different skills of being able to both receive and give love. If your childhood experiences didn't give you many positive memories and experiences of trust, it may be very difficult for you to approach your current relationships with any level of confidence that you will be loved. Because our expectations and our beliefs about our relationships form the basis for how we communicate and behave in them, it becomes easier to see how many people continuously make bad decisions about the relationships they choose.

And yet the story does not end there. Many neglected and not-well-loved children of the world have gone on to heal their belief systems and live out loving stories. I am among them. It doesn't happen easily, but learning the skills of loving is possible. For many of us, the key is learning to believe that we are worthy of love. Having compensated for so many years, we may be experts at the skills of loving others, but until we do the hard work of realizing that "in spite of ourselves" we are lovable, we may never have a moment when our relationships feel secure.

If there is any key to this work it is that love is a verb. Seeing ourselves as lovable is an act of intention that must be a part of every day.

Tending the Hearth: Meditations on Creating an Ecology of Love

Our capacity to love is the source of our genius, the inspiration for our creativity, and the essence of what roots us to the earth. Yet love takes practice; love is an action verb, an act that is skill-based. Seeing our relationships in terms of a practice of love drills is a helpful approach that can keep your heart open and willing to try again, even after the inevitable hurts that define human relating. Rilke said that "the ultimate, the last test and proof of our humanity, the work for which all other work is but preparation, is for one human being to love another." To begin, commit to the truth that you were born to love, and know that you have the capacity to love more skillfully, more courageously and with more tenacity than you ever imagined.

"To be loved, be lovable." — Ovid

The first skill in loving is to believe in your lovability and then act in accordance. Kindness, generosity, and all that is good in us come from this place of feeling lovable. Sometimes just by adopting lovable behaviors, we increase our own perception of our own love-ability. Getting to our own love-ability can be a challenge for those of us who grew up being taught that we are not worthy of love. Many of us have known a time when these kinds of messages hung over our heart like an axe poised to fall. Turning away from these old messages is a contagious practice that benefits wider and wider circles of people. Like any practice, the more you look for what is good, the better you get at seeing it.

"The greatest science in the world, in heaven and on earth, is love." — Mother Teresa

Approach the loving relationships in your life as a cherished science experiment. Think of the universal requirements for success in any loving relationship and objectively evaluate how these are reflected in your own relationships. Do you share enough communication to feel heard and to hear your partner's feelings?

Are you having mostly positive thoughts about the intimacy and process in your relationship? Do you show up for the important, sad, and celebratory moments of each other's lives? These questions are most effective as guideposts. If you know where you want your relationship to go, then answering these questions with intention and action at all times is the active science of loving. It is a work in progress.

"Can there be a love which does not make demands on its object?" — Confucius

Suicide is not the only way to die from a broken heart. There are many more slow, silent deaths around us, as we refuse to love anyone again in a committed way for fear that we will be hurt.

Many of us live with a variety of body aches that transform over time but never really go away. Living in our body demands that we work with our injured muscles and rebuild our strength. Someday there will be a scientific test that can measure the scar tissue in the heart. Just like those of every other muscle in our body, tears in our hearts repair, but not always in an orderly way.

Dealing with the pain of brokenheartedness, which is pretty much guaranteed in loving humans, is no different. Really feeling the sadness and loneliness when love doesn't work can also live in us as deep appreciation for the people we practice loving.

"The day will come when, after harnessing the winds, the tides and gravitation, we shall harness for God the energies of Love. And on that day, for the second time in the history of the world, man will have discovered fire." — Teilhard de Chardin

Here is a prophecy that feels optimistic. With our mandates from the government on renewable energy sources, we may soon be charging our lives with the power of wind, sun and water. So maybe the time has come when we will harness the energy of love for what it is—our access to a fire that can warm us from the inside. Commit to building an ecology of love in your relationship that nurtures the fire of sustainable love. Choose the thoughts that ground you to your love. Communicate and self-disclose what is most difficult to say, and feed the fire with the truth of who you are. Show up in the small details as well as for the important celebrations of living with someone, so that there is always a flow of time and energy between you. Bask in the rare, mysterious alchemy of making love to someone who loves all of you. This is a fire that can and does change the world.

Love and Balance

To lose balance sometimes for love is part of living a balanced life. — Elizabeth Gilbert, *Eat, Pray, Love.*

Sometimes we give up one kind of balance for another. Our work takes over our personal life; new families take over old exercise routines; and sometimes our love life can take over all of it. Losing our balance over love can be fun. Actually that in-love, out-of-control craziness of deep connection can be like a drug, blurring our vision so that the world has a rosy hue and commitments to anything other than our beloved are hard to keep.

Losing our balance when love disappoints us can be just as confusing. It isn't just a partnership that ends. For many people, their basic identity and beliefs about family and promises are shattered. Losing love blurs our vision of ourselves. Keeping up with other commitments during this painful life re-construction can make love feel like a disease.

Sustaining a loving relationship requires remarkable balance. Because no one is easy to love all of the time, thriving relationships not only demand healthy boundaries that respect each partner's individual needs, but also the ability to recognize what is lovable alongside what is most difficult about each partner. Striking this realistic balance in love is daily work and can swing between that rosy, "in love" feeling and that of darkness descending.

This pendulum swing in relationships can be clocked sometimes in as brief a period as minutes. It is not unusual for me to forget how good I was feeling about my mate or marriage only a few days before. Developing the skill to step back and observe your own feelings changing is a useful tool to finding balance. On a good day, the witnessing can create enough space to avoid reacting immediately and give you the time to find the center again, where you can hold the lovable and the difficult side by side.

Lately I have been studying Pilates and doing the physical work of finding balance. Building my core pelvic muscles in this way has deeply changed not just how I live in my body, but also my life. Even better than the end of lifelong back pain is the emotional stability that has come with a newfound strength in my physical center. Working on the body and getting out of the mind is a direct and visceral route to feeling balance.

Living in your center also provides an entirely new and much more exciting access to experiencing an entirely new balance in physical intimacy. Orgasm is the single act that simultaneously releases tension and restores fullness to the mind, body and spirit, creating moments of perfect balance. Finding and maintaining balance in relationship to ourselves and others is worth all the effort it requires. Sometimes it's just a willingness to surrender to the imbalance that sets things right. None of us is perfect, and life is imperfect, too; realizing that helps us to appreciate the beauty in all of it.

Try this:

Although it's not always easy to do in our "driven" culture, make a commitment to find balance in every part of your life—in your thoughts, words, and actions. Pay attention to your feelings and thoughts, and remind yourself of your real priorities.

You Are What You Love

Michelle had worked with John for two years. He was a graduate student, and she was a busy magazine editor who had hired him for a photography internship. She didn't think of him romantically—he was almost ten years younger, and she was too busy taking care of her children, proving herself at work, and trying to heal herself from the pain of her divorce.

But he was always friendly and kind, and he would stop by her office regularly to say hi, share a CD he'd found, or bring her a piece of chocolate. Often during those visits he would tell her of a recent mountain climbing adventure or a camping trip he'd taken with his friends, or a tale from his childhood growing up on a commune. And she'd laugh, and remember her own camping trips and childhood experiences.

One evening she was socializing at a work event when he appeared from another room. "I thought I heard your voice," he said. She laughed—her nasal East Coast tones were a dead giveaway. But that night she dreamed of him, a sweet dream where they were laughing and talking. She woke up with a feeling she hadn't had in years.

Always the professional, Michelle tried her best to hide her growing affection for her much younger intern. And then one night working late in the office, he told her he had noticed. "I have feelings for you, too," he said, "but they're confusing. I find you attractive, but I don't want a serious relationship." Michelle, who hadn't dated in the three years since her divorce, listened to him. And then he kissed her.

They spent the next four days straight together, each time parting ways with no promises. I'm a cougar, she thought—but she was happily in love. She wrote him a note telling him no matter what happened, he had brought her back. On the fourth day, he came to her house and said, "I'm sorry. I shouldn't be doing this with you. I don't want to be serious, and I'm leaving after this internship, and you have children and I'm still a child."

Michelle thought for a minute her heart might break again—she had to admit that she'd entertained the thought of this becoming something more than a fling. But then she smiled and hugged him. Later, she'd shed a few tears for what might have been, but for now, she was happy to realize she could still feel that way.

"You are what you love, not what loves you. That's what I decided a long time ago." I was struck by this concluding line of a five-year-long conversation between Nicolas Cage and himself (when he played the twin writer brothers in the 2002 movie "Adaptation"). I have often reflected on it when hearing the stories of unrequited love that I have heard since then. Cage's character, Donald, knew something that most of us miss, sometimes for a whole life—that the love we feel for whomever or whatever we are feeling it for is our own. Love is not something we are given permission to feel, or a feeling that anyone can take away.

There is a pervasive idea of the experience of love as a coupled experience, its legitimacy resting in its reciprocation. When love is withheld, rejected, diverted, or takes some other form, the one who loved first is belittled, even if only in his or her own mind. Maybe that's why I have always remembered Donald, who couldn't care less whether Sarah, the object of his love, felt that way too. He knew that the gift of the experience was his.

The stories of unrequited love and the range of tragedy and heartbreak from love unmet have filled the airways since we began to sing or tell our stories. The universality of the loss experienced by love gone wrong, or never really given a chance, or interrupted too soon by tragedy, is something we all share. The pain is deep and real. The sadness and loneliness of loving and losing the object of our love can shadow us for weeks, sometimes months, sometimes even years. This is the story that many of us never get over, sometimes keeping us from the prospect of loving again.

Why we can't celebrate the love we feel without it being reciprocated has a lot to do with our latent feelings of unworthiness (don't worry, it's not you—it's the whole culture). As soon as you feel you are "not good enough," the original experience of love, which is the highest feeling we can experience, degenerates to a feeling of shame. Or if we are angry, then it is easy to find blame, making the object of our love not worth the feeling to begin with. Either way, we lose access to the purest and most instructive feeling we can experience.

Realizing that you are what you love, and not what loves you, is a revolutionary approach to opening your heart and discovering a capacity to embrace the world that you might not have known you possess. Loving builds emotional literacy and gives you the courage to feel the loss of love with grace and forgiveness. A loving and compassionate heart begets more love. The more you practice love without shame or blame, the more love comes to you. Guaranteed.

Lovingly Annoying

Elaina and Mick had been together for two years. She loved him, but since they'd moved in together, Mick's small habits had begun to seem oppressively irritating. Like the way that Mick always wanted to read a newspaper during meals—even at a restaurant. He also twiddled his moustache a lot. When they'd first been dating it had seemed like a cute meditative habit, but now it seemed weird and constant and sort of sickening. The things that Elaina loved about Mick—his kindness, his love for his family, his humor—were slowly being obscured by his habit of leaving a full jug of milk on the kitchen counter overnight, and his penchant for buying large boxes of fish sticks and other appalling frozen foods at Costco. How had Elaina not seen these things earlier in their relationship? Had he really just shaved and left dark beard hair all over the sink? What kind of monster was this man?

The truth was that Elaina probably had seen all of these habits in the two years they'd dated. But their living situation illuminated them in a stark and unflattering light. Mick really was annoying, in some ways. But was Elaina annoying too? She considered her stacks of unread magazines and her messy closet, which had all but overtaken Mick's organized one. She decided that she'd try to keep sight of, and hold tight to, the things she knew she loved about Mick—the big, deep things that were the foundation of their love. And the annoying things? There were plenty. But maybe he felt the same way about her, too.

Here's the thing about loving people: They are annoying. I tell people this regularly and they laugh, sometimes a nervous laugh, but more often a knowing laugh. We laugh together out of relief, too—it's not just you, or me, but let's face it: Collectively, we are all pretty annoying. Certainly a look back through our collective human history is nothing if not a testimony to how incredibly annoying we all are—and how little things can turn big, bad and ugly.

Even within our own tribes and families, our similarities and genetic ties are challenging to grasp and sustain. With both partners and children, appreciating how we are related is something that we have to learn and re-learn. It takes separating the essential loveliness of the people around us from all of the incredibly annoying traits that fill the din. Overwhelming our sense of connection are the small things—how people chew too loudly, or talk while they are chewing—the noises we make when we brush our teeth, or the crumbs we leave on the counter, or the socks we can't seem to put in the hamper. In my house, these lists are infinite and trivial though weighty. Learning to sustain our relationships and choosing to stay happens in all the small moments of the everyday mess of life.

Collectively, we are all pretty annoying.

I am struck by just how often and how hard I have to work at loving people and accepting them as they are even when they are so annoying. This is coupled with almost a continuous chorus of people I know who can't quite commit to their relationships, the old one-foot-out-the-door syndrome, because they find living with their partners excruciating. We all want our own space—and our space in order as we would have it—but rarely is that the nature of living with other humans. It all comes down to admitting just how annoying the whole business is and realizing that I am just as annoying (read also: human) as the people who annoy me.

These issues surfaced frequently in my early years of creating a family, and the most important takeaway from our years in marriage counseling was this: If you can hold what is deeply lovable about someone in one hand while holding what is most annoying about them in the other, then balance, patience, and choosing to forgive and love in spite of the difficulty (or annoyance) is possible.

Taking that lesson to the world at large is in some ways more challenging, because strangers by definition are, well, strange, (at least to us), and so holding what is lovable about them with what is annoying about them can sometimes be hard to imagine. I remember a recent conference where I was in the midst of some 30,000 of them. This, even under the best of circumstances, is a lot of strangeness. I strived to see the lovable, but I would be a liar if I didn't admit that I was frequently faced with the challenge of how annoying we all can be.

Among strangers, we face a different list of what separates us: how people dress, smell, ignore us, talk over us or interrupt (one of my big weaknesses as a stranger). Here again, the list can be lengthy. Yet, the results are universal—all of these annoying qualities make it easy to make these unknown people "other" than us. Taken to the extreme, it is not that big a jump to seeing how many of our serious social ills are the unfortunate and increasingly disastrous consequence of our inability to see through what is annoying in all of us.

So here's my proposal. Let's just go forward admitting how annoying and flawed we all are, so that we aren't surprised when living together becomes challenging. We will all go in knowing that we are choosing to get over it, and in doing so, we'll find these brief yet life-changing moments of holding on to what we all want the most: each other.

The Grass is Greener

Kevin had been corresponding with Laura, a former graduate student of his, for months. At first, their e-mails had been friendly reminiscences of their late nights in the biology lab and Kevin sharing professorial advice, but after a few months they'd gotten friendlier. One night, after they'd been trading witty observations about other biologists, Laura shared with him that she'd always had a bit of a crush on him. And, although he hesitated a moment before pressing send, he wrote to her that he'd always had a bit of a thing for her, as well.

His wife, Nancy, didn't suspect a thing for months—she was always asleep when he got home from the lab, completely wiped out from being at home with their two boys, the youngest not yet sleeping through the night (this was part of the reason he always worked late and, he would later rationalize, part of the reason for the affair: he felt like things were exciting again, like he was desirable to someone exciting). She didn't suspect anything when he signed up to attend a conference in Denver, only a hundred miles or so from where Laura had her first teaching job. And she didn't suspect a thing when he disembarked the plane upon his return. She and the boys were waiting for him at the airport, holding a sign that said "Welcome Home, Dad!" Although he'd only been gone for a long weekend, the sign at the airport was one of their longest-running silly family traditions—and the sight of it made him feel like a criminal.

Although he had been sure that his face would give it away, it was his effusive response to Nancy's new haircut that first raised suspicions. It'd been years since he'd noticed any changes in her hair, and this was only a trim. She enjoyed the attention, especially as he'd been so inattentive lately, but she wondered. Later that month, when the cell phone bill arrived, it only took Nancy—a former investigative reporter—a few minutes to figure out that a series of late-night calls to somewhere in Colorado bracketed his trip.

He knew he was caught when she appeared in the door to his study, holding the phone bill. He could see she was trying not to cry, but he couldn't tell whether she was angry or hurt. He'd soon find out the answer: both. And as he considered what he would say to her, the first thing that came to mind was "I couldn't help myself."

If ever an expression defined human behavior, it is the notion that the grass is greener on the other side of the fence. Ovid, an ancient Roman philosopher and poet, was perhaps the first when he said that "the harvest is always more fruitful in another man's fields." This sense that life is better for others has perhaps its strongest and most debilitating hold on us as it affects our relationships. Infidelity, the most cutting breach of trust that we experience in our intimate relationships, is rampant. In fact, it is so common that not having some form of the experience is uncommon. While stories of infidelity are as unique as the millions of individuals who engage in it, the emotional needs and the thinking errors that precipitate affairs are universal.

Humans are not hardwired for monogamy any more than most mammals. The work of David Barash in the *Myth of Monogamy* is a great primer in understanding why infidelity is more the norm than the exception. "We are not naturally monogamous. Anthropologists report that the overwhelming majority of human societies either are polygamous or were polygamous prior to the cultural homogenization of recent decades." In a recent study of committed partners, fully 95 percent of men and 80 percent of women fantasized about sex with other partners.[6]

As if our biological programming were not enough of a challenge, we then add the complexity of human emotions to the mix. While our most basic human need is the need to be loved, valued, and accepted, it does not stand alone. Included with that is the need for power and control as well as the need for competence and accomplishment, to name just a few desires that often impact how we love each other and how we experience the love we receive. Many people report leaving their relationship over unmet emotional needs, which are a stone's throw from the physical intimacy that affairs offer. Given our seeming inability to understand and articulate our feelings and needs, it is not surprising that many relationships end up a revolving door.

Our struggle with the constructs of monogamous marriage that we have created to build and maintain our tribe is legitimate. The truth is that choosing and committing to love someone is not that difficult in and of itself. What becomes impossible for many is that the promise demands that we not choose anyone else, ever. This is painful even in the best of relationships, when someone unexpected and attractive shows up out of nowhere. When your relationship feels disappointing and lonely, meeting a new prospect can easily turn into a point of no return.

Often the moments of intrigue that lead to indiscretion are the moments of least clarity, when we make the common thinking errors associated with affairs. In hindsight, we see how our biology leads our thinking. Added to that, a decision to leave a decent, workable relationship on a whim (or to stay with a relationship that should have never happened to begin with) starts to make sense. Recognizing our inability to see the biological attraction of a fling for what it is can be a place to start when faced with choices that betray not just the people we love, but what we believe about love itself.

Meeting the Need

Rita had been married to a truck driver for a year. She had thought, getting into it, that he'd naturally want sex every time he made it home. He worked the long-haul shift and was gone for weeks at a time. His precious hours at home, she had assumed, he'd want to spend lavishing attention on her—making love, going on dates and cooking dinner. But that hadn't been the way it had turned out.

When her husband Bill came home, he wanted nothing more than to sit back with his feet on the table and watch sports on television, putter around in the garage or backyard, or read a book. And the sex she assumed he'd crave? She'd spend extra time making sure she looked her nicest, but he'd often collapse into bed exhausted, barely noticing. She was certain he wasn't cheating on the road, so what was the problem? Why did she always have to initiate sex? These issues started to turn what had been a house full of loving feelings into a seething cauldron of repressed anger.

She kept trying to do all the nice things she always did for him, like preparing his favorite at-home dinners, but she did them muttering under her breath. She was going to kill him with kindness, and if he didn't want her, well maybe she'd have to divorce him. Thoughts like this invaded her head each time he pulled into the driveway: she had so built up her expectations and felt so rejected that while she still loved him dearly, all her thoughts were toxic. The bottom line was that Bill wasn't behaving in the way that Rita expected him to, and it made her feel unattractive and unwanted.

In the end, Rita had to tell Bill what she was feeling. He was shocked, and said that he worked so hard on the road thinking of providing for her that by the time he got home he was just dog-tired and needed a deep rest. She said they could get by with less money and he could work less, but she just couldn't handle feeling rejected by him all the time. Then they stared at each other in the kitchen like strangers.

She realized that rebuilding their relationship would be an undoing of expectations and hurts, and it might not start in the bedroom. There would have to be more talking, more quality time, and less judgment. She'd need to banish the negative thought patterns and let go of expectations. Instead of being angry about what her relationship wasn't, she needed to start learning to love the imperfect reality of what it was.

Even after 25 years, there are still days when I become angry with my husband for not meeting my (unspoken) needs. These moments catch me off guard. There is usually little warning as I am going along, doing the next thing in my non-stop routine as mom of four and small business owner. Then somewhere in the midst of mailing the day's orders, violin lessons, dance class pick up and shopping for dinner, something snaps in me.

The unfolded laundry, the incessant demands for homework help, the moody response from my teenage son when asked to clear the table—all of this builds into an inner crescendo that overwhelms me. The sight of my husband, sitting in his study, feet up on the desk, reading through a recent *New Yorker*, is all that it takes to send me over the top. Mind you, I haven't asked for help, I just can't stand that he hasn't offered any.

This is a familiar scene in homes across the country, where women don't ask (or are angry that they have to), and men wonder why they didn't. I am mostly over the idea that if my husband doesn't volunteer the help, it is somehow less worthy, but I have many friends who still feel like the love offered in response to a request is less worthy than the same act unbidden. This is a useless, lose-lose way of looking at the situation. Just because it doesn't occur to someone to get up and grate the cheese for dinner really doesn't make the macaroni and cheese taste worse. (Well, I'll admit that sometimes it does, but usually only for me).

This cycle of unmet needs is not limited to my marriage; it creeps into my relationships with my growing children and even sometimes into my friendships as well. Do I really have to ask for the table to be set or the dishwasher to be emptied every single time? On the "unmet needs" days, an offense as small as the children neglecting to put their dishes in the sink feels like parenting failure and a friend's last-minute cancellation of a walk becomes a measure of my self-worth—or lack of it. The little things go from being a blip on the screen of our relationships to defining them, and nothing looks or feels very good to any of us.

I think I may actually be a need-aholic. If I look at the way I have organized my life, it seems that I am addicted to responding to the needs of others. This is in direct contrast to my husband, who rarely has needs that he will voice and is even more rarely seeking random needs of others to meet. Relationships generally involve people with complementary, if not diametrically opposed, needs, which is one of the aspects of relationships that makes them unique and interesting.

It is hard to be needy, anyway."

A friend recently told me, "Your kids don't even know they have the need, and you are already acting on it." Sadly, this is how astute and over-compensating my need-aholic style can be. The mood sensor and stabilizer in me is on constant overdrive, which is helpful in fostering healthy dialogue, averting stupid bickering, and generally keeping the peace with and among children—but it also is exhausting and mostly serves to distract me from myself.

Even after all these years, I am blindsided when I am struggling and unconscious about my own emotional needs. It isn't really that uncommon. Many a competent and seemingly self-contained adult is unaware of the unmet needs that lurk beneath the shiny veneer of "getting it all done."

It is hard to be needy, anyway. There aren't that many places to take your needs that are politically correct. It isn't my children's job to care for my needs, although when my oldest daughter recently e-mailed me a poem from her newly appointed college digs that she said reminded her of me, I wept for what she saw in me.

It isn't my husband's job to meet my emotional needs, either, but I wish he would just think of it sometimes. Or notice how many things got done that he never had to give a second thought. It is a running joke in my family about how I "take the credit" for both big results and menial tasks. Constantly meeting needs anonymously and without notice is an act of devotion that is difficult to sustain, which is why many mothers should be nominated for sainthood. In fact, I realize again that it is not sustainable to be selfless, and actually I am able to do more for others when I am first there for myself.

Unmet needs can wreak havoc on the relationships that hold them, and it is easy to point the finger at the offending partner. But in reality, it is rarely the other person that didn't meet your needs. First, it is most likely you who couldn't recognize or articulate them, and then it is the agreements built into relationships that need to change and evolve with life. It is easy to keep the status quo and then be forced to run from the relationship—and from the resentment and bitterness that comes from never adjusting and re-balancing.

It is more challenging to hold the relationship accountable for meeting some of everyone's needs. This actually provides alternatives for healing needs that have been long unmet. We are able to renegotiate our relationships when we shift the blame and guilt from the other people involved—to look at our needs, to ask for help when appropriate, and to forgive those we love for their inability to hear what we are not saying out loud.

The Heart's Memory

Gretchen waited for her turn by the pay phone at the emergency room to call her daughter. Again she had found Roger in the kitchen, muttering to himself about an enemy invasion and pacing back and forth, slamming things on the counter, tearing at his hair. As always, she had calmly gathered her car keys, purse, and coat and taken his hand—he spun wildly, ready to defend himself, and she ducked. "Let's go, sweetheart, I'm taking you to the hospital," she said.

He was still in a frenzy, but he recognized her voice, and it brought him back enough to get into the car. He was having one of his manic episodes, she knew. They had been through this routine at least a dozen times since the war.

Other times it was worse, like the time she found him in the bathroom with his wrists slashed, or the time he'd been up all night, phoning his congressman, the CIA, the FBI, and anyone else he could think of to share what he kept muttering was "the ultimate solution" or when he'd just slide into a funk and not talk to anyone, or bathe, or sometimes even eat, for weeks. The doctor called it bipolar disorder; others diagnosed it as "extreme shell shock." The accounting firm had let him go and he was on permanent disability.

Many times, after one of these episodes, the doctors had suggested hospitalization—and sometimes, when the episodes were more than she could handle, Roger had stayed a week, two weeks, even a month in the VA hospital. She'd visit him daily, after work, bringing him cookies, a slice of pie, some books. His face brightened when he saw her. He told her jokes, and she held his hand while they did the crosswords together.

She knew that people sometimes whispered in church when they came in together. Her closest friend had asked whether she should have him permanently committed. And she hated it when people said things like "I don't know how you do it." She had a good life, couldn't they see? Three beautiful grown children, a home, a good job that she loved (she'd had to go back to work full-time). She saw her friends, took cooking classes—there was nothing about her life she'd change, other than Roger's suffering. Sure, they wouldn't get to retire and see the world like they'd talked about when they were kids, and that made her sad, but they had so much—and she hadn't skipped over the "for better or for worse" part when they'd married. This was simply life. She looked at him in the hospital and all she could see was the boy who had asked her to dance so long ago, the father of her children, her husband.

This, was
simply
life.

There are different kinds of loss—the loss of dreams, the loss of "what might have been," and the loss that comes from life's hardships. I have generally not been a sports fan in life, but living with my husband for more than 25 years and raising two sons has trained me in the importance of "the game." Recently, we shared a real loss as we watched the dreams of a star quarterback slip away with an injury to the knee. He stood on the sidelines watching his team lose their chance at a national championship. This is the game of life we watched play out on television—the winning and the losing that defines our lives. I always tell my boys, especially after they lose, that you can't ever win if you don't risk losing. The losing is what makes the winning real.

We can never imagine the full range of possibilities that can befall us in the games we play or the relationships that we live in. Our imagination is limited by our experience, and we shape the future pictures of our lives by what we hope will happen, rather than what could likely happen. It is often the thing that you couldn't imagine, that you don't see coming, even when it is barreling down on you like a linebacker, that ends up to be the defining moment. Not being able to accurately predict our future and the outcome of the game is what makes life so exciting and risky.

The players will return home and figure out how to try again. Married couples will adjust to a picture that's not quite as they'd imagined. To go on, they will have to be willing to take the risk again. Losing in private, when no one else is watching, is not a lot easier. Finding the courage to try again in the game of relationships, careers, or athletic endeavors depends on our ability to access our heart's memory.

It is through our heart's memory, the place where we remember gratitude, that we find that what we have is enough and that we are enough even when we fail. When we experience gratitude for both our own efforts and the efforts of the people around us, we can come back from our losses with courage. This grace is the energy that is able to turn denial into acceptance, chaos into order and confusion into clarity. We realize that being in the game is enough, even when we are left with less than a golden win.

Consider being thankful for your heart's memory—the inner store of loving thoughts and connections that has given you the courage to keep going. Communicating your love is the essence of gratitude. And gratitude is the essence of turning a meal into a feast, a house into a home, a day into a celebration—and a marriage filled with struggle into one that can still be filled with love.

Cultivating Love

Max stood at his son's soccer game, cell phone to his ear, away from the crowd, one eye on the game while he negotiated a contract for his client to buy another shopping center. As he often did, he had slipped away from his daughter and his wife, who were in the stands cheering along with the rest of the parents, as they did for every game.

The deal was just about done, there were just a few more details to work out and he could call the client and claim success.

The game ended, and he was still on the phone. He could see his son, high-fiving his teammates before running over to his mother and sister and daughter. Max began walking quickly toward the car, hurrying to finish the call just as his son arrived and jumped into his arms for a hug. "Did you see it, Dad? Did you see my goal?"

He hugged his son tight and lied "Yes, I saw it! It was great." His wife gave him a knowing, sad look—it was a look he'd seen before. Anger and indignation mixed with guilt as his phone rang in his pocket—his client. His family got into the car, waiting to go for pizza, as they did after every game. "C'mon Dad!" his son called. He'd call the client back once they'd ordered, he decided. And he did, and he missed half the dinner.

That night, he crawled into bed long after his wife had read to their two children and gone to sleep. They'd exchanged words in the kitchen as she poured their son a glass of milk. "You didn't even ask me how the deal went," he'd spat. "Don't you realize I'm doing this for us?" He was ready to fight, ready to defend his role as breadwinner, until he saw her face. She was crying. "You should have seen it," she said. "He was so excited. And the first thing he said when he got to the stands was "Where's Dad?"

He lay in bed, mulling over the next day's to-do list, and feeling lonely. He looked at his wife as she lay sleeping—she was such a great mom. He got up and looked in on his son and daughter, both sleeping peacefully. He decided right then that he'd be home for dinner—and he'd leave the cell phone turned off until the kids went to bed. And maybe, once he'd apologized, he'd talk to his wife about taking a trip somewhere, just the two of them—or maybe all four of them could go to Disneyland. It didn't have to be this way, he thought. He didn't have to be this person.

While many might scoff at the suggestion that love can in fact reinvent our world, recent scientific advances have proven the effects of love on human consciousness. According to doctors Thomas Lewis, Fari Amini and Richard Lannon of the University of California in their groundbreaking work, *A General Theory of Love,* "Who we are and who we become depends, in part, on whom we love."[7] Through careful explanation of brain development and the wonder of being both mammalian and neural beings, their research demonstrates that humans have the capacity for "neural revision." This capacity provides the power to remodel the emotional parts of the people we love. Long-lasting togetherness actually writes permanent changes into the brain's open book. Our relationships pull us into our loved ones' emotional life at the same time as we mold them to our own.

...love can in fact reinvent our world...

This fact is both a gift and a burden, because unlike the technological efficiencies that our modern existence has come to depend on, the life of the heart and its relationships lives on in time. Relatedness is a physiologic process that, like digestion or bone growth, cannot be rushed. The skill of becoming related to another person and attuned to that person's emotional capacity and rhythm takes years and requires continuous attention. Relationships are always in process and require the same amount of attention in midstream that they do in the beginning. Single moments of disconnection wedged between hearts can and do turn into weeks, months, or years of distance.

Relationships die every day from inattention and neglect. Many couples cannot love simply because they don't spend enough time in each other's presence. People mistake text messages and e-mails for togetherness, yet screen exchanges or even a voice over a line lack the life-connecting substance of time spent side by side. If this is true for adults working to sustain their relationships, it carries even more weight for the developing hearts and limbic brains of children. There is no substitute for the daily presence and attention that families offer the next generation. If any single thing is ailing our culture, it is this: the utter disconnection that broken families leave in their wake, while children are left to learn for themselves how to connect and build lifelong relationships.

Family is the foundation that community and culture is built on. Resolving to give the relationships that make your life meaningful their due is a gift that you give not only to the ones you love and yourself, but to the entire culture we collectively create.

Forgiveness: The Action Verb

Nancy took a deep breath as she stood in the door to Kevin's study holding the phone bill. She was wild with emotion—anger, hurt, resentment. "How could you?" she cried. They had been together for five years before they married, and, while she had been "the other woman" when their relationship began, she never thought that he would cheat on her while they were married. She was reeling, and she didn't wait to hear his answer before she heard herself saying "I want you to pack your stuff. You want to be with her that much, so much that you'd manufacture a conference and spend our money to fly and see her, if you'd risk your family and our home for this woman, then—then just do it."

He didn't pack his stuff, so she did: After calling a divorce lawyer, she packed her two boys and the contents of her home, rented a house, sight unseen, over the phone, and prepared to move out.

"That's just like you, Nancy," he said to her one day, after they'd quarreled over who would keep the cheese grater. "Don't you even want to talk about this? Or is it just going to be like all of your other relationships, like with your mother." She cringed as he reminded her—she had moved halfway across the country rather than deal with her issues with her mother.

Kevin continued. "This isn't a pattern I want us to repeat with our sons. I'm sorry. I screwed up. It just… it felt so good to be needed again. To be desired. I hadn't felt that in a long time. …"

He trailed off, because she had started to cry, hard. He came and took her in his arms. And then he said to her "I'm human. I know you are, too. Can't we just be human together?"

She wasn't ready to forgive him. She moved out, and for almost two years she lived in a rented house about a half mile away from him, gritting her teeth when they would meet to drop off or pick up their sons. Kevin didn't move to be with "the other woman." He went to work, and he showed up on time for all of their appointments, and he paid his child support regularly. In time, it felt OK to have dinners together once in a while, like the family they were. They still liked each other. And then her counselor asked how she felt about Kevin's infidelity. "You don't even seem to be considering how you feel about it," the counselor said.

She was angry, hurt, and afraid—and after some additional counseling work, she was ready to admit that Kevin's infidelity had reminded her of the same abandonment she felt as a child. She cried, buckets of tears, in her counselor's office. One day at dropoff she told him "I am so angry with you. I can't believe you would do that." He looked at her and simply said, "I'm sorry."

Nancy began to look forward to their weekly dinners with their sons. Maybe, just maybe, they could rebuild.

> To forgive is to set a prisoner free and discover the prisoner was you. — Unknown

If love is a verb, then forgiveness is the action verb. It is the highest form of love and the single behavior that most distinguishes our human potential. In an ancient tale from the Kabbalah, God told some angels in training that the capacity to forgive is the most excellent gift in the human experience, more essential to the continuity of life than the courage to sacrifice your own life for someone else, or enduring the pain of giving life. God explained to the angel "Forgiveness is the only reason my creation continues. Without forgiveness, all would disappear in an instantaneous flash."

Forgiveness is giving up the idea of having had a better past. It is the path of redemption where life can move forward from the present moment, where the past fades with memory and we have the grace to accept the daily imperfections of life with those we love as they are. It is a true forgetting, this forgiveness that frees the victim as deeply as the perpetrator. The relationship is new, starting fresh, without the burden of selective memory. This is not a path that we command; it is one that we serve.

Forgiveness does not come easily, and for many it is an unknown. It requires patience and is rarely a hasty proposition. It cannot be forced, but it is a way of thinking that has to be chosen. The most arduous and sometimes insurmountable part of forgiving is that one must fully feel the injury and acknowledge it before anything can be forgiven. This is why so many families of origin never heal. Children don't have the language and emotional maturity to express themselves. The parents, often suffering with their own unresolved childhood pains, have little insight into the damage they have done. As a parent myself, I often and painfully bear witness to the enormity of the task; even with my best intentions, I often fall short. It is impossible not to inflict some harm on the way to raising another human being.

Some children may spend years in therapy trying to understand, and later forgive, their psychic injuries. Where my family of origin is concerned, I have been working toward forgiveness—which has been called the final form of love—for much of my adult life. I knew it was a real and promised place from my experiences in transforming my marriage. Still, at every family reunion it has eluded me. Inevitably something in me cracks, destroying the tentative approach we are all trying to make. I haven't had the heart to love the most broken places in me that are so vividly mirrored in these interactions.

As all of us age, each visit with my family of origin also has the potential for being the last. I long for the freedom to open my heart in these moments, but mostly am faced with all of my worst and ugliest character traits that are mirrored (and amplified) in the previous generation. As I witness the source of all my most unwanted behaviors, the ones that stick to me regardless of how much or for how long I keep them at bay, I understand finally that all of this brokenness is not about them any more; my brokenness is mine alone. Still, these traits that I know intimately bring up a deep revulsion in me.

But there is also a glimmer of goodness as my father teaches my son about the stock exchange, a piece of my own education that has stayed with me for decades. He starts recounting stories from his own broken childhood that I remembered fragments of, but now I get the missing details, the names and places that made him who he is. Tenderness catches me off guard around my father. It has rarely been safe to have my heart unprotected near him. I sit, waiting to serve forgiveness, to have the chance to be free of the years of "not good enough" that I lived.

Tenderness catches me off guard around my father.

It is thanks to my own family that I can inch closer to the edge of forgiveness. My eldest son, who knows me well and is unaffected by my father's offenses, told me the other day that he thought "it was refreshing to hang around Grandpa. He has no idea how he affects anyone else. It's funny." I can see his point, but stubbornly remain protective of the small girl that I was at the receiving end of his apathy. My son acknowledges how that would have "sucked" to be the kid—and something softens in me.

This is perhaps how forgiveness happens; a few strands of a thick cord tying you to your hurts are worn away through the courageous process of feeling and acknowledging, until you can see that the injury holding you has less to offer you than the freedom of carrying your brokenness tenderly on. It is the only real beginning.

Most of us struggle with hurts—real and imagined—that separate us from the ones we say we love. These can be big hurts, like infidelity or another kind of betrayal (and forgiving may not always mean staying together), but it can also be the little things that we hang on to that do us damage. The smallest of details in sharing a life with someone can easily turn into a negative story line about the person you love. For years, my disregard of my husband's need for order and cleanliness, and in turn his disgust at my *laissez-faire* approach to house cleaning, came to mean everything. We weren't talking about behaviors where we dramatically differed. Instead, each housekeeping incident became a personal insult that with just a small push inflamed us to fury about the other weak points in our relationship.

In *Meditations*, Marcus Aurelius said "our anger and annoyance are more detrimental to us than the things themselves which anger or annoy us." The petty arguments of life are the cracks in the foundation of our relationships. Left unresolved, they often fall into the established patterns of retreat and attack that impact the ability of both partners to be emotionally available and vulnerable.

I have only experienced the deep, life-changing balm of forgiveness in my life once. Right at the moment when my marriage hung on the precipice of its end, we decided instead to forgive. I can't say who initiated it or even exactly how it happened; all I can say of that moment is that I couldn't remember any longer what it was to not be wanted. All the years of fighting over who we weren't for each other evaporated; what was left was a space to love someone for who they were. My intimate life, very much at the core of my marriage, was reinvigorated with a curiosity and genuine interest that had been obscured by our relentless arguments. I was blessed. I have, since that time, tried to remember just how that could have happened and how I can reproduce it.

I think that forgiveness is an act of the imagination. It embraces the child's heart, which is always ready to risk for a better moment and give up the hurt of the last one. Forgiveness is an innocent place where your hurt and pain does not have to have the final word. There is little that has more power to transform the world than the courage to bear witness to your pain and then let it go.

CHAPTER 3
Learning to Swim

Many couples struggle to find a balance between too much structure

and too much flow in their time together. For some couples, togetherness accentuates other elements in the relationship that aren't working.

During the early years of our marriage, we built a life with enough distance to allow our unspoken conflicts a space to live between us. Most of what I remember during that time is the weight of loneliness. This is not uncommon: Feeling lonely with someone you believe is supposed to make you feel loved is, in my opinion, a root problem in many relationships.

Learning how to be together in a life crowded with responsibilities and children takes time and patience as well as an ability to experience and surrender to loneliness. Many help columns talk about the importance of setting aside time to go on special dates and really focus on each other. While this kind of special time is helpful and can give any relationship a boost, it can't replace the core of what it means to feel "together" with your partner in the trenches of life.

Humor and kindness are the keys to sharing a life and experiencing the feeling of togetherness that helps one maneuver through it. It is well documented that being able to find the humor in what might otherwise be a stressful situation is not only good for your physical health, it is essential to the well-being of your relationship. Laughing over spilled milk or "breakfast for dinner" served three nights in a row can sometimes be the most loving thing we can do. This playfulness carries great mileage for exhausted parents and partners in all areas of life.

Equally important is practicing kindness in the small exchanges of life work. It is easy for new couples to slip into nasty habits, where sarcasm and "I'm only kidding" barbs pepper the conversation. These bad habits eat away at the trust and intimacy that take so much energy and time to build. Ask yourself if you would ever speak to a friend (or even for that matter, a stranger) the way you speak to your partner. If not, realize that the tone of voice and the gentleness that you bring to the smallest of exchanges will go miles in sustaining a relationship that is safe, trusting and intimate.

Try this:

Have more fun with the people you live with and love. Laugh at spilled milk, burned toast, or breakfast for dinner. The most damaging things that happen in our relationships are not the actual things that happen, but how we relate to and communicate about them. A sense of humor can add strength and depth to your ability to love someone.

Two Feet In

It was much easier to keep one foot out the door. That way every time Liesel's partner disappointed her, she could easily imagine an alternate life with another partner, in another, possibly warmer place. She could leave Tyler and take up with some gentle carpenter in Tucson, and they would live in an adobe house overlooking the desert, where there would be lots of sex and magical summer rainstorms. By keeping the fantasy of escape alive, it made it easier to deal with the often dull and daily disenchantments in the lives of two computer programmers in the rainy Pacific Northwest. She did love Tyler, in a deep and tender way. It was just that he wasn't perfect, and sometimes she wondered if she could have a much better, more exciting life with somebody else. This sort of secret twilight of commitment hovered over their lives for years, until Liesel became so disenchanted that she actually left.

Her escape-hatch fantasies failed to come true. After three weeks in Tucson she missed Tyler terribly, and she realized that she had been systematically destroying her relationship one half-baked fantasy at a time. It wasn't Tyler that she needed to leave, it was the illusions of perfection that she had allowed to poke pinholes into her marriage. A commitment with an even theoretical escape hatch that was visited on a daily basis was one that was bound to fail. She drove her Subaru back to the Pacific Northwest. It was raining, and Tyler was still the same guy she had fallen in love with. She resolved to stop letting doubt eat away at their love.

I don't remember the exact day that I pulled the one foot that I had out the door back into my marriage, but I can't remember the last time that it occurred to me that I would ever leave. It seems like I should remember when that change took place, as it so profoundly changed the very fabric of our lives together, but like most things in life that happen in small increments, we don't see them as they are happening. They are only clear as we look back.

My husband and I never had a fairy tale marriage. In fact, anyone who claims to have one is probably neither present nor honest. Our love for each other was uneven, and the common sexual issues of attraction and initiation—who wanted who first and who wanted who more—plagued our ability to connect for years. The classic "I'm not in the mood" or "I'm too tired" responses create a cycle of defensive and offensive reactions that are almost like a pre-patterned dance. It's a scenario that many couples just don't have enough vocabulary to escape.

In hindsight, I know now that there is no winning side to that argument, but whichever side is most familiar can color your lens so completely that the other side seems like a holiday. The shame of rejection is really no better than the guilt of turning away. The pain is equal. I have read that the rejecting partner is the more powerful of the two, but having been on both sides, I don't think it's true: Both sides leave you unable to connect and feeling powerless.

Two things transpired in my marriage to lift this issue and allow us to experience sexual desire without the burden of fear and unmet longing. The first one was choosing my relationship without reservation. Being in my marriage with both feet in the door, I had a lot more balance and flexibility, which gave me more room to deal with the issues that had been keeping me distant and disconnected. When I gave myself permission to truly stay, rather than to be looking for the reasons to leave, it changed my relationship to both the issues and my husband.

True surrender is when you have no memory of how things were before. The past loses its grip, and suddenly there is room for a new way of relating. It's an odd phenomenon, because it isn't an experience that you can will to happen. It is something that happens to you, seemingly without you, when you have an open heart and the intention to find out what there is to stay for. Choosing to stay in a relationship is tied to the belief in the power of forgiveness to change life completely. It is the singular pathway we have at our disposal to make things new between people.

Having an excellent memory and the need to be right are not helpful in developing this quality in your life.

The other important change was that we made an important agreement to stop saying anything mean or disrespectful to each other. Becoming conscious of the words you use in your daily relating is the door to making a partnership safe.

In my case, with practice, the hurtful ways we communicated were supplanted by the two of us actively trying to stay. Over time, even the negative unspoken thoughts we were trying not to say were replaced with small kindnesses. Connection happens by itself when we feel safe.

Seemingly suddenly, we began exploring our intimate life with a whole new curiosity and openness. Our sex life became the glue to hold the more challenging places together. The safer I felt in the relationship, the more risks I could take in the bedroom. The more our physical love flourished, the more our relationship thrived. There are still times when one of us might not feel in the mood when the other does, but now it doesn't mean anything more than what it actually is—bad timing.

Although it took us years to get here, sharing the kind of deep intimacy that is the reward for years of communication work that you put in together is an extraordinary blessing. There is nothing like the power of loving someone who loves you back with their eyes wide open. There is no place in life that is more satisfying, healing and transformative. It will take your breath away.

Go On Anyway

Do not let the fact that things are not made for you, that
conditions are not as they should be, stop you. Go on anyway.
Everything depends on those who go on anyway.
— Robert Henri

Sometimes words can help you find the courage to go on anyway,
to be willing to come back again and again. I realized this one
day as I realized how much I struggle with maintaining a positive
mindset toward the challenges of running a small business, that
really, if I could just apply the hard-won lessons of how to sustain
a relationship to my work, it might feel totally new—or at least
doable.

Learning how to stay when things are difficult in families is great
practice for working though obstacles to other dreams. In the
same way that I would never think of leaving my family, even at
the most painful of moments, I long to have that same whole-
heartedness for my work.

A lot of us live with one foot out the door in some area of our life,
whether it be personal or professional. The thought lurks behind
every setback: I don't have to stay with this. I could be happier, if
(fill in the blank). For me, these thoughts don't happen much with
my partner or my family anymore. Yet they are a recurring theme
amid my dreams of building a meaningful love business. This
is definitely not good for employee morale and damaging to the
efforts sustaining a vision.

I remember the years that "the foot out the door" was true in
my marriage. This safety hatch actually is a silent destroyer.
Relationships and dreams are not safe if failure and setbacks
become the justification for endings.

Thomas Edison said, "I have not failed. I have found ten thousand
ways that won't work." It is this kind of commitment to a process
in building a relationship, a business, or a dream that allows you
to find the way to the light. Keeping one foot out the door does
not allow you to ever fully give yourself to the process that can
take you to the other side.

Doubt is not a leader. And yet, doubt surely leads many of us away from our real desires and our sense of purpose. I think we don't realize how we are all on the verge of making the slight changes in our life that would make all the difference. We are not quiet long enough to hear the courage in a quiet voice at the end of the day that says "I will come back tomorrow and try again." We give up too easily on ourselves. We are afraid to trust our own efforts as being enough.

The question of quitting or staying is always a question of love. Trust in the strength of our own heart to keep going, while all the time being willing to fail. Know that your heart is strong and resilient enough to try again.

Try this:

People change; even people you have loved forever. Always think about building your relationship so that there is enough room for both you and your partner to explore more of yourselves.

Promises We Keep

Tracy and Michael had moved in to a tiny cabin in Northern California, with big trees and the scent of eucalyptus in the air. Those years were flush with happiness—they reveled in each other's presence, walking hand-in-hand to the local grocery store to stock their little world with provisions. They rarely wanted to leave each other's side.

Then they were married. They traded their little cabin for a house in the suburbs of San Francisco and jobs that came with desks, titles and health insurance. Children came next, two beautiful ones named Matt and Molly. The years accumulated. Tracy began to glance sidelong at Michael and not recognize him. A Regional Manager of Sales with a paunch and an unquenchable thirst for televised sports games had replaced the young, bearded man chopping wood for their cozy cabin. She remembered the butterflies she felt when he walked through a doorway back then. She began to feel pangs of dissatisfaction where the butterflies had once been. It didn't feel like it used to.

When they had married, on a foggy day north of the city, they had made a promise to each other. But wasn't love always supposed to feel like love? She thought about the intervening years, the years in which Michael had worked his way up to Regional Manager of Sales, cracking her up at night with impromptu comedy routines featuring his diabolical bosses. They had laughed to the point of tears. She remembered the baseball games they'd gone to as a young married couple, the way Michael leaned over and kissed her every time the Giants scored a run. She thought of their home, the way they had moved into an empty, blank slate, and the way it was filled with children's toys, vacation photos and anniversary gifts now. Maybe all of this was what love turned into after time: years of shared experience, a relatedness that they didn't have when they were living in the little cabin in the hills of wine country. Back then, their relationship was pure and strong, overwhelming at times in its intensity. Like wine, their relationship had aged and mellowed. She realized that she was in stage two of love. The lump-in-the-throat newness was gone, but it had been replaced with a new and complex flavor, a relatedness only built with years. First, she had a hunger for him. Now she had relatedness. And the bridge between the two was her promise.

A promise is a commitment you make with your heart. Promises are not like other decisions that we make that have open-ended options of easy termination if we decide our choice doesn't suit our needs or doesn't make us happy. The act of promising releases the right to reason on some level, because keeping a promise requires us to go beyond reason. Staying true to our word in spite of the inconvenience and discomfort is the core of a promise.

In the days of Camelot, the Knights of the Round Table made a vow and were sacramentally knighted. They knew their promise was sacrosanct. While there were moments of romantic adventure, they were signing on with their lives for whatever ordeal the promise would demand of them.

Loving someone carries this kind of promise. Different from the heady falling-in-love stage or the romantic whirlwind of a love affair, committing to authentic love that lasts is an agreement to give up our own personal simplicity in exchange for the continuous yielding that creates and sustains relationships. This long-term commitment to love is also an ordeal of sorts, one that changes the participants each time they agree to keep loving.

Keeping a promise to love is a lifetime of saying yes to your relationship. When it works, the partners understand that they are not really giving to each other, but rather to the relationship, which makes the sacrifices of personal satisfaction life-building rather than impoverishing.

There are all kinds of commitments in which we make this kind of loving vow. Marriage, parenting and devotion to a career path all provide a context which require us to go beyond the "reasonable" and to give more than we believe we can. It is in these crises that the promises we make are the light at the end of the tunnel. Sometimes, even now after 25 years of marriage, the best reason I have for staying is because I said I would.

Promises are hard to keep for two reasons. Coming up with the constant willingness to stay put and do the work is an act of faith and courage that we don't always know how to find. In addition, it is often long after we make a promise that we realize that our promise to one person or situation precludes our availability to everyone and everything else. Choosing a specific career path means closing a door to so many others. Committing to a partner precludes this kind of intimacy with all the other intriguing people we meet. A huge world of possibility closes with each promise we make.

It is **heroic** work to make and keep a **promise.**

This may be why there were only twelve knights at that Round Table. It is heroic work to make and keep a promise. It is not for the faint of heart. What most people who quit on their promises don't know is that the moments when it seems impossible to say yes one more time, or the weight of the commitment is unbearable—those are the very moments when your promise has the most to teach. Each time you pass through this threshold with your integrity intact, the promise and the love grows large enough to hold whatever else wants to break it down.

The Gift of Presence

When it's over, I want to say: All my life I was a bride married
to amazement.

I was the bridegroom, taking the world into my arms.

— Mary Oliver, "When Death Comes."

I was thinking about this during the busy holiday season this past
year. It's easy to get so lost in the momentum of activities and
the seemingly endless to-do lists that we forget what the holidays
are for. There is always more to do than there is time for, and
probably never quite so acutely as during the holidays. Gift giving
drives a lot of the frenzy, and although we can point to all the
cultural mania driving us to exchange dollars for good feelings, for
many of us there is a legitimate desire to give something that feels
meaningful and is a true reflection of our love.

Every now and again we are fortunate enough to know of a
particular thing that is truly desired. Better still when we have the
exact make and model number. However, short of those golden
opportunities where the desire matches our ability to give, there is
precious little that we can offer in the way of material goods that
can communicate our deepest feelings. The power of advertising
further complicates this by making us believe that certain gifts
will speak volumes about our love—diamonds, flowers and fine
chocolate are a few that come to mind.

While those are all nice gifts, I don't know if I have ever gotten
a more authentic sense of my partner's love for me than when
he has taken the time and gotten over the inconvenience factor
to show up for me. Some years he has shown this by helping me
wrap gifts late into the night for our four kids. Other holidays, it
was drawing a bath for me and reminding me to give myself
the attention I so readily give away to others. Or sometimes he
would make a romantic bed by the fireplace. The best gifts have
always been the moments of him giving himself. The gift of
presence is what we all want most: to know that we are not alone
in the world.

Sadly, it is often at the most tragic moments in our lives that we experience the gift of true presence. In moments of loss, the details that consume life fall away and we realize that the mystery of our frail human form and the relationships that make life meaningful are all that we have and all that we ever really had. This gift of pure presence is not an easy one to live in. In the moments of pure love and connection or pure loss and loneliness we know that our emotions are not thoughts in our head, but weighty forces that fill our physical body so completely that they have the power to alter our senses.

Falling in love is a full-body experience, one that alters how we see everything; there's no more powerful drug on the planet. The same is true for grief, especially grief that we don't allow ourselves to experience. Feeling the weight of our own sadness is frightening. There is no deeper emotional access to the present moment than our sadness and grief. Yet feeling the full force of these emotions often reminds me of my kids when they were three years old, just old enough to feel their experience but without a big enough body to contain it or a language to express it. Witnessing the trauma of a full-on tantrum is enough to make any sane adult choose to repress it. The power of those feelings is as great as any force of nature.

Here's the truth: It doesn't work to repress our feelings. Our experience of life demands to be witnessed and shared. All that is not aired will like any force of nature so transform and alter our internal landscape that we can't find our presence—neither with ourselves nor with the people we long to love the most. Giving yourself or someone you love this gift of pure presence is the most amazing and life-changing gift you can offer.

Eternity is not waiting to happen after you die. It is happening right now—and the meaning and love that you have the chance to make in your life is the only gift that will really count when your days are over. So instead of just exchanging physical gifts during the next holiday season, open your arms wide to the stories and feelings that make our presence real and our relationships sustainable.

Take the Time

Elise remembered when time seemed like it would stretch on forever. It had a very specific feeling: Like standing on a peak in the Oregon Cascades and looking out over the endless trees, feeling diminished by the landscape. She and Steve had been living together, in an old tumbledown house full of cobwebs with peeling linoleum floors in the kitchen. They were in their twenties then, and they spent evenings drinking beer on the back porch. Steve liked to nap in the hammock strung between the trunks of two gnarled cherry trees. Life was good, mostly—they were poor and ate a lot of beans and rice, but they had each other. Still, Elise was impatient for real life to begin. Careers, marriage, children, a real house of their own, a vegetable garden, the end of a peripatetic existence of leases and moves.

Ten years later, she looked back on those days and ached for them. It seemed so bizarre and so unfair that she had spent some of their time together—that precious time—being annoyed or angry with Steve, at where they were in life, wanting what they did not yet have, not reveling in what they did have. Steve, who took the hint and did become her husband, had died of a heart attack at 38 years old. Time seemed so different now, and every moment of that beautiful stretch of their lives that she'd wasted being unhappy or worried or angry at Steve was like a burr under her skin. It was so cruel, she thought, that only the clarity and loss of death had forced the realization that the smallest moments were the most valuable ones, and that the endless vista was in no way guaranteed.

"There never seems to be enough time to do the things you want to do, once you find them. I've looked around enough to know that you're the one I want to go through time with." Jim Croce's last love song, "Time in a Bottle," still brings tears to my eyes whenever I hear it, the truth of it becoming clearer with each passing year.

Almost every great love story shares this common theme of the brevity of love, whether it lasts for a year or fifty years. The moment you become deeply grateful for the gift of love you share with another person, the more fragile and ethereal the love becomes.

What if today were the last day to talk with someone you love?

I am reminded often of "the tender intervals in this perpetual departure." A recent news story about a tragic accident resulting in the untimely deaths of young musicians in our community reminded me again of the fact that we never know the last day we will have with someone, the last smile we will share, the last hug. Even without tragedy, I bear witness to this impermanence, which is the essence of life.

The cliché of seasons passing and time slipping away has never felt as real as it did when I helped my oldest child prepare to begin a life on her own. I wondered how I could have missed enough small moments to have this rushing sensation of "where did the time go?" Where are the days that seemed to stretch out endlessly in front of me, the periods of time when life would just drag on? They are gone now. As I have finally realized the brevity of it all, I could just kick myself for the time that I wasted on petty small arguments, impatience over minor incidents, and all the other dozens of ways that we give away our most precious gift—the time we are given to love one another.

What if today were the last day you had to speak with someone you love? What would you say? This is a good exercise to try sometime when you think you can't stand another minute of whatever it is that is driving you crazy with another person: Take a minute and try to imagine your life without them. I have practiced this often, maybe too often, because sometimes even as I am leaving those I love most for a short time, I can often get teary imagining what I didn't just tell them.

I don't want to lose any more of the small moments, so I try not to get distracted by the noise and the clutter of our busy life. I work to stay focused on what is essential. I am pretty sure that the only thing that fits in that category is love. Each time I leave my family, I say "I love you" in as many different ways as I can imagine. Just in case, I want it to be the last thing they will remember from me. Although I don't know for sure, I believe that at the last moments of our life, we remember the love. Don't take the time you have for granted. Love as much as you can while you can.

Benefit of the Doubt

Geneva worked as a middle school counselor at a low-income middle school and spent her days functioning as a cross between a therapist and social worker. She cared deeply about the kids and gave a lot of herself, constantly organizing fund-raisers to help struggling families buy school supplies and clothes and cooking dinner for kids she knew were being mistreated at home. She was the woman who'd make a pot of soup for the neighbor going through chemotherapy, who'd hear about a grieving widow across town and visit her for tea.

While she had no problem giving (and giving, and giving) to her community, Geneva had a bigger problem giving to her husband, Doug. She found herself being short-tempered and resentful toward him. While she could look past the faults of the people she served in her professional life, his were huge and glaring. Doug had been unemployed for several months, and Geneva felt herself welling with anger every time she encountered him relaxing instead of looking for jobs. Didn't he see everything that she was doing?

One day Geneva was talking to a mother of one of her students, a recovering drug addict who lived in transitional housing with her son. This woman had made a lot of mistakes—some so big that Child Protective Services had gotten involved—but Geneva felt for her. This woman, with her methamphetamine-scarred face and worried, bitten fingernails, was just trying to do the best that she could. She seemed to be trying to make a go of it, and Geneva felt she deserved the benefit of the doubt. On the way home, seething after a phone call from Doug, she thought about her heart. Why was she so willing to give this woman—a relative stranger—the benefit of the doubt, but not as willing to open her heart to her imperfect but loving husband?

Here's a resolution that anyone can keep: Give the people you love, starting with yourself, the benefit of the doubt. Generally speaking and almost without exception, most of us are doing the best that we can at any given moment. We are being as loving as we can be, as kind as we can be, as generous as we can be, even though our best might not make it, even (and especially) in our own eyes.

This was brought home to me in a deep and personal way as I spent the holidays with my family of origin. Although there was no storming out, door slamming, or other traumatic arguments that might suggest the end of the relationship, what remained made the reality of the relationship clear. It was bittersweet, this realization of what was left between us and our mutual agreement not to try to be understood or to initiate a reexamination of all the old wounds.

My fifteen-year-old son commented that my mother did not bring out the best in me. He loves his newfound wisdom, and I could not argue the point. Sometimes the love we can express doesn't bring out the best in us, and although we may wish to be kinder and more loving, the reality of the past and all the baggage that is primeval in us means only the benefit of the doubt can protect us.

It is a humbling realization, to see clearly the limits of one's own capacity to love and still try to come to a place of loving oneself. This is actually our only choice. In the words of Martin Luther King, Jr. in his speech "Where Do We Go from Here?" this "creative redemptive love" is "ultimately the only answer we have as a human family." This redemptive love, which is far from the way we idealize loving relationships, is what we are given to build family and community. It has to be enough.

With many of the people in my life, loving them brings out the best in me. I am inspired to give generously of my time and resources. It is comforting and easy for me to accept even my weaknesses when I am with these people with whom I share a heart connection. I don't have to think about the benefit of the doubt so much in these relationships, because they make me feel strong and, on good days, confident.

But until we can embrace the relationships where we are weakest, (and sometimes meaner than we want to admit), we can't fully embrace the rich heart connections. All those parts live in us, and they can't be neatly categorized by the quality of the relationship. In fact, the more complex the relationship, the more likely that the benefit of the doubt is the only thing that can sustain us.

Showing Up

Janine was getting ready to leave for book group when her husband, Michael, called from work. "I have to finish this project," he said. "I'm really sorry, Jan." She knew how much he wanted to be promoted, and how much was riding on his performance at the office. But in truth, she was growing weary of calls like this, which meant she would either scramble to find a sitter, which they could ill afford, or cancel her plans—again. "Not tonight," she barked into the phone. "I canceled last time, and if I'm not there it means I'll have read the book for nothing. Again. Can't you just bring the work home with you?"

"I'll see," was all he said. "Let me call you back."

After she hung up the phone and wiped away the tears that were rising to the surface, she headed for the phone to call a sitter. On the way, she passed the shelving unit for her son's room sitting in the hallway. It was almost complete—Michael had stayed up late the night before to assemble it, stopping only when he realized he was missing an essential part. She stepped into her son's room with a different thought.

"Let's go," she said. "We'll get Thai takeout and visit your dad at work."

When I teach about the Ecology of Love and talk about the water that lives between people, I often use the term "showing up" to describe the flow that happens in relationships. In relationships, like the ocean, there is an ebb and tide to how we are present for each other, but if the water in the relationship is always out, then both people feel alone more often than they feel there is someone at their back. Many people in partnerships go through years in partnerships in which the experience of loneliness is profound. It is something that I struggle with in my own marriage, with each of us having a different sense of what togetherness means and how much of it we need.

Showing up for someone doesn't necessarily have anything to do with long, deep conversations. In fact, it is usually in the small details of life where showing up makes the most difference. The day I got a flat tire and my husband came and changed it in his nice work clothes, or the time when he needed a shirt washed and ironed in a hurry and I dropped everything to do it, or the zillions of times when the kid juggling isn't quite working and he has been willing to stop what he is doing to pick up the slack. It communicates volumes of love when you are able to give up your own agenda to show up for someone else's needs. It is at the heart of what it means to feel safe and loved in a relationship.

It is easy to confuse coexisting and showing up. They can look almost the same when we grow accustomed to not allowing ourselves to need and be needed. Coexisting doesn't have the stickiness factor that showing up does, because it happens as a matter of course, not choice.

It's easy to
confuse
co-existing
and
showing up.

Showing up or not translates into all the dynamics of a relationship, including how and what you communicate and whether you share a passionate physical love. It isn't possible to really open yourself up with either the spoken language or one's body if you don't feel safe. Instead, we say less and less of what we really need to say, and in our most intimate times we protect ourselves through distancing and not really being present.

Here's another important point about showing up: Don't keep score. It doesn't balance like other human equations might, and only serves to undermine the ground of the relationship that you are trying to build. The point here is that each person shows up when he or she can, and that both people know when it happens. When it does, be grateful and reciprocate.

Life Cycle of Love

Mary and Dan had been together for 25 years and married for 20—and life was good. Their youngest child had just left for college on a soccer scholarship, and Dan was in the process of buying out his retiring partner in their dental practice. Mary had good friends with whom she walked every day. She raised money for the women's shelter in her community and occasionally took on work as a legal consultant, something she had done from the time they were first married.

At first, as she walked around their empty home, she thought the creeping sadness she felt was only loneliness for her children. Dan hadn't changed—steadfast as always, he was home for dinner every night, mowed the lawn on Saturdays, and called out "hello, beautiful" every time he entered the house. But Mary didn't feel beautiful. She felt… nothing. When she looked in the mirror, she was plagued by her short grey hair and about ten extra pounds, and when she woke in the morning, she saw a day before her that was just like the last one: walk, do some volunteer work, check in with the kids. She couldn't face twenty more years like this. She couldn't tell Dan—loving, consistent, Dan—he would just want to fix it, and she didn't want to trouble him when he was so busy re-organizing the practice. Besides, she didn't know how it could be fixed. But something needed to change.

It isn't just you. An international study of two million people from more than 70 countries confirms what many of us have always assumed: the happiest times in our life span make a "U," with the "up times" early and late in life. In the middle of the dip is middle age.[8]

Researchers from Dartmouth and Warwick found this to be true across cultures, regardless of income, marital status, family size or job satisfaction. Middle age consistently makes up the bottom of the curve. It is a time when happiness and satisfaction are hard to come by. This phenomenon is unexplainable except as something deeply human: Middle age can be a challenging time of coming to terms and making peace with life.

Perhaps it is as incomprehensible, yet true, as the tumultuous adolescent years that pull us down while pushing us forward on the trajectory that becomes our life. Relationships reflect this life cycle. Early love relationships carry an urgency and immediacy that supersedes all else in life, regardless of the outcome. The experience is nothing if not life lived to its fullest. We invest ourselves completely in these first forays into love; we allow these relationships to transform us.

The mid-life dip is real, and it takes a serious toll on our primary relationships. We find ourselves overwhelmed with competing agendas, including but not limited to concerns for our environment, communities and political issues, initiatives to eat better and exercise more, the exhausting joy of raising children, trying to be our own personal best, the cost of living spiraling ever upwards, and our tired, aging bodies all converging in days that just aren't quite long enough to fit it all in.

I am in the mid-life dip club—big time—struggling every day to give voice to the reasons to stay, to keep loving, to not let the bad moods take over and dictate my life choices. Bailing out of love feels as if it would be easier in this time. Maybe it is easier, and yet I know leaving the foundation that I have invested in wouldn't get me any closer to the peace in myself that I so long for.

This becomes clearer too, both in the study statistics and in the day-to-day, as we move toward the latter part of our life. When we finally give up the struggle and the tension of defining who is right or less imperfect, there is nothing left to be taken for granted, least of all the time or comfort of sharing a history with someone. We know finally what this life is for; the slower we go, the more that love is the only balance worth striving for, the only path with enough heart to help the rest of life make sense.

So wherever you are in your life cycle, recognize your relationship as the perfect mirror for this time. If you are in the wild throes of falling in love, thank your lucky stars and spread the love by sharing the constant smile that only that particular emotional state can inspire. Feel the intensity in every cell of your body so that you can create the memories that will get you through the mid-life dip.

If you are still lucky enough to be loving someone who has seen you through the highs and lows, treasure it and share it.

If, like me, you are knee deep in the mid-life dip, then imagine your relationship and your capacity to love as tools to stretch out the curve and soften the bottom of this bumpy life transition. Remember the intensity of the love you invested in during easier times and bank on it now. Even if you can't always feel it, the initial investment is still there. Take the time out of your busy schedule to listen, take a walk, or have a physical conversation. Reach forward in time and realize how golden this will all feel when you look back on it. Admittedly, sometimes I can't imagine it ever feeling golden, but I do know that there is a tenderness and connection that will heal the bruises of moving through hard times.

Love is a Direction

It is only necessary to know that love is a direction and not a state of the soul. If one is unaware of this, one falls to despair at the first onslaught of affliction. — Simone Weil, *Waiting for God*

Something snapped in me tonight. I didn't see it coming, although the fog of exhaustion and the kink in my low back should have warned me. I should have gotten take-out, left the laundry in the washing machine, taken a half hour to lie down, but instead, I moved through the daily list of chores, attending to the pets, the kids, and the house before myself. Then like a tornado spinning up from nowhere, I was screaming: All of the grievances that I usually keep neatly filed for discussion at some later date flew out of my mouth with a force and fury that shocked even me. So much for a nice family dinner: The tenuous peace with my teenage son, who often simultaneously wants everything from me and nothing to do with me, is hanging by a thread again.

Perhaps I can blame this breakdown on my simultaneously raging and disappearing hormones. According to many accounts,[9] I am not alone in my unprecedented exhaustion, flaring temper, and inability to focus. But even if there is a sound biological reason and legitimate bad chemistry for my mini-breakdowns, the fissures in my relationships that go with them are mine to mend. Claiming brokenness does not get you off the hook; we are all broken in some way.

Knowing that love is a direction and not a state of the soul is sometimes the only ground I have to stand on, especially when I am overcome by a biology that is reinventing itself. My feelings of being "done" are as real as my commitments to love my family, and they wrestle in me, continuously seeking balance or at least solace. I don't really want to give up on the promises that I made earlier when I was flush with regular hormones and seemingly endless energy. I want to learn how to keep the promises without losing myself.

A dear friend once told me that "your boundaries are how you love yourself." This is uncharted territory for me and millions of women who grew up associating who we are with whom we love and how well we are loved. My new biochemical mix forces me to find what is mine alone and honor it. For many people, this time ushers in the end of many old relationships and promises.

I don't want to believe that relationships have an expiration date, although I have heard the concept more than once of late. Not infrequently, I have to defend my position that we don't know what a relationship has to teach us if we don't stick around through the painful, conflicted, and difficult stretches. One friend recently told me that six weeks is long enough to know if someone is capable of loving. Our ensuing argument was a testimony to the different kinds of pain that we each choose for ourselves. I am not convinced one is better than another during the painful parts, but I keep choosing to learn how to stay. Each time, the connection in my relationships only deepens. I need to have someone on my side in life, even if I can't feel it each and every day. Recommitting to relationships, even when you don't want to, is the art of sustainable love, which requires great humility and courage.

T.S. Eliot once wrote: "For us, there is only the trying. The rest is not our business." We cannot guarantee our results in life; we can only step forward with love as our direction and hope it is enough.

Three-Dimensional Relationships

When she thought about it, Jane had to admit that she and her husband had fallen into a routine she wouldn't have chosen. Home from a long day at work, she and Max ate takeout or some soup she whipped up in a hurry. Often, with dishes still on the table, they sat at the dining room table with their "friends," —a combined 400 of them—each on their respective laptops, sometimes catching up on work, but mostly reading their friends' news on Facebook. At one point, they laughed because they were actually "chatting" while sitting across the table from each other. Sure, they were together—laughing over YouTube videos of their nephew's antics, responding to comments about their latest status updates. She rationalized that in spring they'd get out after dinner and take a walk, but right now it was too cold and dark in the evenings, and at least they were more or less talking to each other and not watching television.

But the routine was also killing their sex life. Usually one of them would tire and head for bed while the other stayed at the table just a little longer, fingers tapping on the keys. Even during the work day, they texted each other rather than calling to say hello.

It was when a friend posted photos of her three-year-old son on Facebook that it hit them both. "Wow," Jane said, look how big he has gotten! We haven't seen him since his second birthday party." And Max responded "Yes. His parents were our best friends in graduate school. And they live less than a mile away." Jane unplugged her laptop and put it in her bag near the door. "I'm leaving this at work from now on," she told Max. He agreed. The next night, after dinner, they took each other's hands and walked the nine blocks to their friends' house in the rain.

With all the discussion of economic crisis going on today, there is little recognition of the even deeper poverty of heart, which, like a creeping malaise, impacts the very core of our well-being, our life and the meaning we derive from it. Recent studies by the National

Opinion Research Center at the University of Chicago found that, throughout the last twenty years, more than one in four of us have no one with whom to discuss important life issues or to confide in, compared to only seven percent in 1985.[10] Loneliness doesn't get much airtime because it is still so stigmatized. Many people cannot distinguish loneliness from depression or anxiety and feel that to describe themselves as "lonely" would be to identify themselves as a social outcast or worse.

Actually, loneliness has more in common with the physiological human functions of hunger, thirst and pain. The impulse for social connection, which is built into our neural wiring, is rooted in the basic urge to survive. We are not wired to live alone, researchers say. "The need to deal with other people is so great," says John Capiocco, author of *Loneliness: Human Nature and the Need for Social Connection,* "that, in large part, it made us who and what we are today."[11] Most neuroscientists agree, according to Capiocco, that it was the need to process social cues that led to the expansion of the cortical mantle of the brain. And yet loneliness grows in the midst of more ways to "connect" than we may have ever imagined twenty years ago.

This is in large part due to the confusion we all share about what constitutes real relationships. The "friends" and "connections" that we may be adding up online often serve only to distract us from the few real friendships and intimate connections that fill our three-dimensional time. It is easy to see how this happens. Our busy lives, combined with the ease with which we can conduct those two-dimensional relationships, favor them.

Real relationships are three-dimensional. They use all of our senses and exist in real time. This is not unlike the difference between playing basketball on a screen or getting out and using your whole body. The real game is intense and can be demanding. We are wired to play and relate with our whole being. The people who share your kitchen, your bedroom and your heart are the ones who make your life whole and full. Yet they also often require us to give of ourselves in ways that make us stretch and grow.

The same three-dimensional comparisons could be drawn about our sexuality. The numbers of people who pay for two-dimensional sexual contact are staggering. Virtual sexuality carries none of the physical benefits of the act in real life, and it often leaves you feeling lonelier than when you began. While the secrecy and clandestine fantasy that virtual sex affords might titillate, it will never heal.

Demand the real thing in your intimate life.

Demand the real thing in your intimate life. Don't give your life energy away to a computer screen.

If the economic crisis has any upside, it is that it might just make us more aware of the wealth of friends and loved ones that have gotten lost in the speed and intensity of life in the fast lane. Shifting your energy back to the heart of your life relationships has the power to re-invent how you spend your time and how you think about your life goals. Reach out to the people in your life that you may have only been texting and share a meal. Call and chat with an old friend that you haven't spoken with for a while. Re-focus your days with true three-dimensional relationship time, and enjoy a lasting stimulus in your life work.

The Life Force

Charlene worked the swing shift in the ER at the local hospital four days a week from noon to 10:00 p.m. Her husband, Greg, worked in construction, rising each morning at 5:30 to be at the jobsite by 6:00 a.m. This arrangement was wonderful for their family life—Charlene was always available to wake the kids and take them to school, and Greg met them by the flagpole as they ended their day, got dinner and homework handled, and had everyone tucked into bed by the time Charlene got home at about 10:30. By that time he usually could muster only a mumbled "Hi honey," before relocating from the couch to the bed. It took her an hour or two to unwind after a ten-hour day, so Charlene usually stayed in the warm spot he'd left on the couch watching TV before slipping into bed with him. They both worked hard, and they were both tired, and they had an unspoken contract that they'd catch up on their lovemaking on Saturday and Sunday mornings while the kids watched cartoons in the family room. But during the week, she sometimes missed her husband, even as they were discussing the kids' homework needs and playdate plans on the phone from her work. She felt like their lives were compartmentalized into weekends and workweeks, and she missed that deeper connection.

One night, without telling him, she decided to try something: rather than staying up and watching Leno, she followed him into the bedroom. Forget Leno—there could be no better way to unwind than this. It didn't take much to convince Greg. From that night on, she made going to bed with her husband a priority. Some nights he still fell right to sleep while she snuggled up next to him with a book, but either way, this became her favorite time of night—something they both looked forward to all day.

Sleep is our most basic human need. Some thirty million of us will attest to the impact of insomnia on our well-being. Unlike hunger, which humans can survive for weeks, being deprived of sleep can kill you in days. The impact is so severe that it not only precipitates physical disability, but also insanity—which it is why it is one of the cruelest and most inhumane torture methods ever devised. Considering that complete lack of sleep is fatal, it is not really a stretch to realize that overwork and fatigue are responsible for a wide variety of illness, injury and disease.

Under the best of conditions, maintaining loving relationships is one of life's biggest rewards and challenges. Many of us don't realize how exhaustion affects our relationship skills. The patience to nurture the bonds of intimacy in our relationships is often one of fatigue's first victims. The struggle between sleep and sex is a common one for most couples in long-term relationships. Tiredness is one of the most commonly cited reasons for not being intimate. The ability to rest and rejuvenate is at the essence of our vitality.

With or without sex, the act of sleeping with someone you love is a bonding act in itself. The soft sweetness of shared quiet and the silent moments of drifting off to sleep with someone dear nearby is healing. More than sixty percent of Americans share their bed with a significant other, and, although sleeping with a partner can sometimes challenge your ability to sleep, more than two-thirds of those polled said they prefer sharing a bed to sleeping alone.[12]

Having shared my bed for my entire adult life, I know the problem solving and conflict resolution that goes on about sleeping habits; who joins us in bed, the weight of the blankets, the amount of light in the room, the window open or closed.

How we work through this most intimate part of sharing a life is a deep reflection of our relationship. The most successful sleeping arrangements, like the most enduring relationships, rely on sensitivity to each other's needs and a willingness to compromise. Sleeping next to my husband, even with the accommodations we both need to make for it to work, is the most extended time I share with him daily. Even asleep, we reconnect and recharge the places that keep us together.

Giving up sex for sleep is a good idea when just lying side by side is all you have in you. But if this becomes the routine, we lose the powerful source of vitality that comes with a meaningful intimate encounter. Sexual energy that is stored in the body is a force that can be used to revitalize even the most exhausted among us. Often times I have been cajoled into intimacy when I thought I was too tired, only to find myself feeling better than I had in days.

Here's an idea: Plan ahead for your intimate times when you are not tired. You will create the mental space in your day to both conserve the energy for your rendezvous and anticipate with revived memory how great it was last time.

Prioritize sex with the person you love as highly as basic hygiene.

As you begin to get tired in the evening, put away the laptops and leave the dishes in the sink, if you must. If you agree to shut the bedroom door even by 10:00 p.m. each night, the chances that you might have a great time and a reasonable amount of sleep are pretty good.

Prioritize sex with the person you love as highly as basic hygiene. You wouldn't go a week without a shower. Even if the main event isn't a daily experience, the compassion and interest you show your partner daily leaves room for this to happen. Be nice and understanding about the need to sleep, and realize if you are sleeping side by side, it's a win either way.

In Sickness and In Health

Mark was frustrated. In the three months they'd been married, Karen had been to the doctor twelve times. "I don't know what it is, exactly—but something's wrong," she said. Karen hadn't been like this during the seven years they were dating before they were married. But now Karen—Karen who had climbed Mt. Baker, Karen who could swim 100 laps before 7:00 a.m. without blinking—called in sick to work at least twice a week and didn't want to be touched. She didn't want to do anything except go to the doctor and wait for tests, or search the web for information about her symptoms. "I'm scared," she said one night in tears. "Scared it's something awful." Hugging her, Mark sighed. He was starting to think that maybe she was a hypochondriac and was tired of begging off on weekend plans with friends or canceling at the last minute because she wasn't feeling well. She could sense it, too: "I'm sorry you married a sick person," she cried one night.

But then her doctor called: she'd found an elevated level of something-or-other in the latest blood tests, and would Karen be available for a CAT-scan the next morning? He held her hand and tried not to think about what the co-pay would be as they waited for the results. It would be nothing, he thought, crossing his fingers that this was the grand finale to what for him was an unnecessary drama.

It wasn't nothing, but it was treatable—a pituitary tumor, which was not life-threatening but would need to be managed with drugs. Mark thought this would end her suffering. Instead, Karen's doctor visits were replaced with trips to the pharmacy, and the time spent on the internet was now spent in chat groups for people with the same condition. Mark would leave the room, if he was home, but mostly he just spent more and more time at work. He wanted his wife back. They were supposed to climb Mount Hood later that summer. The doctor had said she'd be fine—what was taking so long? She still wasn't herself. He hadn't signed up for this.

One day at the office his mother called. She didn't usually call him there; usually their family chats were reserved for Sunday afternoons. "I've been thinking about you," she said. "How are you two holding up?" Mark launched into a tirade of complaint and frustration. His mother listened for a while, and then she said: "I know how you feel. Your father's Crohn's disease took over a year to diagnose, and then it was all we could think about or talk about. I think I was so scared to lose him, and I didn't know how to help him, and so I began to avoid it—and him. Meanwhile, imagine how you would feel: the poor guy was scared, struggling, and feeling guilty for being sick."

On the other end of the phone, Mark started to cry silently. He didn't usually cry—they were a stiff-upper-lip sort of family. His mother knew, though. "You know, I don't want to butt in, but I think I know something that will make you feel better," she said. "Get off the phone with me and go home and hug your wife."

If love is so healing, why does it hurt so much? This is a good question with difficult answers. Love, the verb, is a constant practice of feeling compassion, giving the benefit of the doubt, and remembering to feed our goals and desires, as well as those of the people we love. This aspiration is a struggle even in the most functional of relationships, and the score rarely comes up even.

Approaching our intimate relationships with intent is realistic, albeit a bit daunting. The romantic version of the verb, the measure we use for our love relationships, reflects the illusion of love as a vacation. We sit side by side in some beautiful natural location and the love that we feel washes over us, filling us, just as easily as the nearby waterfall washes over and fills the streambed. Physical intimacy carries the potential to generate this experience; flush with heightened hormones and released tension, lovemaking seems to encompass all of what is love.

These peaks of love are profoundly healing and sustaining; however, it is unrealistic to expect that these experiences should encompass all that is love. When we are unable to show up for those we love, the feelings that we bear are the polar opposite of what we feel when we succeed. It doesn't matter if the sleight is intended, a consequence of life's competing demands, or the result of our own issues. Generating the love sometimes is our work alone.

Life frequently tests our ability to forgive the intrusions to our peace of mind and to sustain the pain and longing of someone we love and cannot show up for. We must be willing to balance the hardships and bear the ache in our heart and in our relationships. If we are unwilling to sustain the work of love, all we ever get is a brief glimpse of a paradise, fading fast enough that it is easy to dismiss.

Illness is as much a part of our human condition as is wellness. The times that we feel most fragile are made more bearable when held in love. Unfortunately, the courage and intention to sustain each other during the daily annoyances as well as the bigger traumas, like major illness, is sadly often more than we can bear. The number of people who report feelings of relief at the end of their long-term relationships continues to amaze me. Loving each other is the hardest work we do—and what we do with that work defines our lives, "in sickness and in health."

Loss and Losing

All goes onward and outward, nothing collapses,

And to die is different from what any one supposed
and luckier.

They are alive and well somewhere,

The smallest sprout shows there is really no death,

And if there ever was, it led forward to life,

And does not wait at the end to arrest it,

And ceased the moment life appeared.

— Walt Whitman, from "Song of Myself."

There are many different ways to lose. Sometimes it's a small
thing that at the moment seems big—like not winning a contest
or getting a promotion—and sometimes it's a pivotal life event,
like the death of a close friend or a divorce. Either way, although
these events are as natural as breathing, we resist accepting them
entirely, or we characterize them as bad. To do so is to lose
the lesson.

I think about the summer Olympics in 2008. My family enjoys
watching swimming. When the camera would zoom to the
winner's face, for some reason I would always search around
the edges to see the utter despair of the losers. Here I use the
word loser almost as a joke; all of the athletes worked, sweated,
and traded their lives to be among the best athletes: they are all
winners. The actual "winning" in these races was often decided
by tenths of a second or less. One swimmer lamented clipping
her nails the night before—the contest was that close. A hundred
years ago, they would have called it all a tie, which is probably
closer to the truth.

One of our most significant human frailties, I believe, is our
devotion to the winner—to winning—or to polarities such as
"good" and "bad" outcomes. An ongoing conversation in my

home, inspired by the ongoing sports and musical competitions that make up my children's world, goes something like this: "There is no losing when you have given everything you have, when you have tried your best." (Actually, it's not really a conversation—it's more like me repeating it as a mantra.) For me, the win is in their courage to play and in not giving up on themselves. The rest is the game, luck and the direction of the wind sometimes. But this is little solace as the other player or team goes away in celebration.

This is true in our careers, in our relationships, and in just about everything we do: Our personal best is not always enough.
Yet to live our lives and to keep taking risks, it has to be. This is a difficult lesson to absorb whether you are 12 years old or 112 years old, but, like the Olympic swimmers, we must keep practicing it until we have it mastered, and we must be ready to shed a few tears in the process.

I was a finalist recently for a "Women in Business" competition that is sponsored by a nationally known clothing line. Months of entry forms, phone calls, e-mails, and waiting led to disappointment after coming so close to being a "winner." Upon hearing the news, I suffered a loss of perspective, self-esteem and general sense of direction—I was angry, disappointed, demoralized.

Later that day, I walked with my friend who had lost her husband about nine weeks earlier. On our walk, she recounted a recurring nightmare that she had throughout her marriage that had recently returned. In the dream, she would be somewhere with her husband and he would disappear. This was a reflection of what happened to them frequently in real life when they traveled together: Her husband was full of wanderlust and even in the midst of big foreign cities would often forget to look back for his wife. She told me that when she had the dream recently she realized that now, just as in life, she had to forgive him, let go of him, and find her way home by herself. We wept.

The losses of life—large and small—that crack your heart wide open and leave you looking at the world broken-hearted are a gift, if only because it is in these moments that we realize all the petty disputes that can dominate our life and relationships mean nothing. We are awake and realize we have another day to tell someone I am sorry or better still, I love you.

As we are sadly, and too often, reminded, we never know the last day.

As we are sadly, and too often, reminded, we never know the last day. So act like today is it. And say all the "I love yous" that have been waiting to fall from your mouth. Give in, give up all that matters least and instead do what we're put on this earth to do: love.

C H A P T E R 4 ˙

Taking a Breath

Communication is the breath of life in relationship. The flow of

communication, not unlike the ebb and tide of togetherness, has its own patterns and includes everything from eye contact to the words we say and the messages that we hear. Individual differences in communication styles (including ability and comfort level) can be where the dance of relationship is most interesting and vital. However, this is often the first place that relationships break down.

Consider what messages you send without saying a word. Do these messages invite your partner to listen, to express his or her opinions and thoughts, or to close down? Unspoken communication, through body language and facial expressions, sets a tone that even babies understand. An atmosphere conducive to real communication must first feel safe to everyone in the conversation.

Listening is a gift of bearing witness that we offer when we love someone. It is a gift that we can only give when we withhold judgment and access our true curiosity and desire to know the other person. In this place of understanding, communication becomes connection.

My marriage transformed when I finally understood this and stopped waiting for my partner to be the kind of father or husband that I wanted him to be. I stopped judging him for not behaving the way I thought he should. For the first time in a long time, I was able to witness who he was as a father and a husband, and I could see him as the friend he had always been. I saw again what I had always valued and admired in him.

So here's an idea: Ask yourself if the way you talk to your partner is at least as kind and generous as you speak to a friend or a stranger. If not, stop and excuse yourself so that you can reconsider your words and find a respectful and loving way to ask for what you need. A mature love requires not only that you balance and hold in your heart what attracts and repels you in your relationship, but that you take responsibility for how you communicate and do so with kindness and respect.

Conversations We Keep

Melissa and Tyler had been married for two years and did not yet have any children. Melissa wanted badly to start a family immediately; Tyler wanted to wait for his business to become established, something that to Melissa seemed amorphous and a long time off. This area was a black hole in their life—it seemed that it could not be discussed. Each time they tried, Melissa became shrill and accusatory, and Tyler became silent and nearly comatose. They both ended up staring at the walls of their living room, sitting on far sides of the couch, and sleeping in the same bed without touching each other.

This was not the way that an otherwise happy, functional married couple should be communicating, Melissa knew. And even her job as a counselor—a professional listener—somehow left her without a clue as to how to fix the ugliness and futility of their conversations.

Somehow it was Tyler who brokered a détente of sorts, before one of their "meetings," called by Melissa, who clutched a glass of red wine and felt on the verge of tears even before she sat down. Tyler stopped her mid-sentence as she told him about yet another friend who was pregnant, and how she didn't understand what they were waiting for. He gently asked: Did Melissa agree that they loved each other? Yes, Melissa did. Did Melissa agree that they wouldn't try to hurt each other or accuse each other of anything? Well yes, of course Melissa did. Did Melissa agree that love was not always easy, and that sometimes it meant putting the other person's interests before one's own? Come to think of it, that was exactly the definition of love that Melissa had always believed in. They made a few simple agreements about what they both believed in, and there were tears. "OK," said Tyler. "Let's talk about this, for real this time." And when they did, something had thawed.

There is an extraordinary power and grace in communicating authentically. A few critical instructions are essential here. First, stop repeating or making up a story—that is, don't let what you think you know (or even what you don't realize you think you know) create assumptions about what is happening. Pretend that you are a reporter, objectively describing an event. Don't attach the event to a lifelong history or previous behavior. Bear witness to it as a singular moment in time. Does this change your view? Experience a brief moment where judgment is suspended, and you might just see a situation with fresh eyes.

There is an extraordinary power and grace in communicating authentically.

Second, don't react. There are times when we react automatically. These reactions often occur before we are even aware of our own feelings. Moving away from reactivity requires time and space. The first response is the one that lives deep inside of you, that has been in your memory since you had a memory. It might not be the thoughtful response that has grown in you during all these years of building a life of your own.

A good way to create the time you need to develop a thoughtful response is to actually take a deep breath. Feel it going in and going out. Remarkable what can change internally with even three small breaths.

If your relationship to your partner feels fragile, or for that matter if your relationship to yourself feels fragile, make agreements before you enter the larger conversations about what you believe about love. This is love in the largest sense—because if you are walking into a conversation where family does not have a shared definition of love, then it is easy to quickly feel lost and alone. This is fertile ground for losing connection to one's own beliefs, or the connection to your partner, or worse still, to yourself. Making and keeping your agreements about love and how you communicate will not only transform the larger conversation at the dinner table, it will transform your life.

Wired to Connect

June and her boyfriend Larry lived together in a house near the beach in Maine. They had met just out of college and had already weathered plenty of storms in their young relationship. Now they'd moved in together, while Larry worked at an outdoor gear store in town and June worked as a substitute teacher. It was a laid-back lifestyle, but June often felt lonely. The move to Maine had been Larry's idea, and when the summer frenzy of kayaking and barbeques ended and the bitter winter winds set in, June felt as if she was surrounded by lobster fishermen and ice—and nobody to relate to. Larry, on the other hand, seemed totally content reading books in front of the fireplace in sweatpants and socks.

So June turned to the glowing screen of her computer, e-mailing and Facebook messaging old college friends, one in particular. His name was Matt, and he lived in New York along with most of June's other college buddies. They exchanged comforting inside jokes and witty barbs, growing closer with every snarky message, she felt. Winter got colder and June spent more and more time chatting online with Matt, whom she hadn't actually seen for years. Their conversations lasted deep into the night after Larry had gone to bed. She felt so much closer to Matt than Larry, and found herself absentmindedly nodding and continuing to type while Larry tried to engage her in conversation or entertain her with stories about his day's craziest customer. He was increasingly a stranger to her.

It took Matt telling her about his new girlfriend for June to realize she'd been living in a world that didn't really exist. Connections didn't really happen on screens. They happened in flesh and blood life, in grocery store visits and walks through town, in sex and in the conversations Larry had been trying to engage her in. Not on a screen.

We finally have the scientific equipment to verify what we have always known: Our drive to be social, to be connected to each other, is actually hardwired. Our need for connection and drive toward empathy is not a result of environmental influences but rather a function built into the brain itself. Daniel Goleman, Ph.D. a *New York Times* science writer and bestselling author of *Emotional Intelligence,* has taken his research to a whole new level with the publication of *Social Intelligence.*[13] Advances in neuroscience now allow scientists to observe brain activity of humans in the act of feeling. They can now witness that we are continuously forming brain to brain bridges—a two-way brain traffic system. In the same way that we can "catch" a cold from someone, we can "catch" his or her mood—bad or good. The significance of the relationship indicates how deeply we are affected and will stimulate actual physical consequences: a hormonal response that magnifies stress (cortisol) or induces happiness (oxytocin).[14]

Positive interactions and being surrounded by loving people actually work like vitamins for your entire being. Negative relationships and interactions don't just make us angry; they make us ill. As in other brain functions, this one also reflects our amazing neuro-plasticity. This is to say that our brains are continually building new connections—and no matter how young or old, anyone's personality can be affected by other people. We literally heal each other through our social connections.[15]

This news couldn't come at a better time, as we continue to replace real interaction with techno-driven reality. Is it really dating when it is virtual? Are we really connected to others when all we are sharing is words on a screen? More than any new technology, what we truly need is to develop a lifestyle that encourages deeper human connection.

Overwhelmed with digital connectivity, we easily become oblivious to the people surrounding us. How often have you witnessed someone at a checkout stand, absorbed in conversation on a cell phone and entirely oblivious to the person standing in front of her?

Real, intimate connections don't happen on the phone, in a text message or on IM: they require a real-life presence where we pay full attention to the people we are with. Empathy grows in our brain through eye contact, voice recognition, and touch—all of the time-intensive ways of knowing another person well enough that we can't objectify them. Empathetic connections are the prime inhibitors of human cruelty. Scientists agree that the survival of our species depends on our ability to grow and develop this innate ability, as well as a culture that encourages deep and true human connections.

So next time you're feeling blue, turn off your electronic gadgetry and go for a walk, preferably holding hands with someone who loves you.

Clearing the Air

It was bad before it was good. Shea sometimes thought that it was crazy that she and Peter ever got married, because they had so many awful problems when they did. Shea looked back and wondered how her bridesmaids, in whom she'd confided about all the silence and strangeness of her relationship, managed to stand next to her and watch her promise her life to Peter. In truth, they had never understood how to talk to each other. They shared a simmering attraction and a deep tenderness for each other, but their communication was a mess. Shea expected words and didn't get them; Peter had no idea. Shea became clingy and needy because her self-esteem was low and got even lower every time she thought that Peter understood something—that she didn't want him to take his brother on their weekend vacation, that she was uncomfortable around his parents—and then found that he was oblivious. They talked plenty, but it was always about the mundane daily tasks of their life—what to have for dinner, whether the Red Sox game would be any good. After they married, the air was so clouded and thick with unspoken desires and frustrated emotions that Shea could barely stand to be in the same room with her husband.

It took courage on Shea's part to start talking, but she knew something had to give. She'd been told—by her culture, by self-help books, and by her own mother—that the worst thing a woman could do would be to force her husband to talk it out. She expected that she'd seem needy, that a woman needed an exorbitant amount of self-disclosure and a man would be sure to shrink into his shell at the mere suggestion of it.

This turned out to be untrue. She finally talked about what she needed, and Peter listened. For the first time she felt good and strong about her role in the marriage.

Wind power is one of the fastest growing alternative energy sources available. What could be cleaner than capturing the power of the moving air and turning it into energy? This is a powerful metaphor on a personal level and in our work to make relationships sustainable.

The air in your relationship flows from the communication that passes between you and your partner. It has the power of a wind generator, and is the source and fuel for physical intimacy.

First,
we must
trust
ourselves.

Taking into account significant gender differences in communication styles and comfort levels is an important beginning. Women communicate with about ten times the number of words as men. Knowing this fact will hopefully allow for differences, without letting anyone off the hook.

People need to stretch themselves when it comes to learning to communicate. Our willingness to share of ourselves in breadth, openness and depth reflects our ability to be intimate. Self-disclosure is literally a breath of fresh air for many relationships, which limit most conversations to dealing with the mundane tasks of managing a life. It is easy to fall into this place where discussions remain on the surface; our busy lives often leave little time to process our own feelings, never mind the complex work of expressing them.

Having conversations of depth requires not only time, but trust. First, we must trust ourselves. Low self-esteem is hard on relationships, because we cannot really build a bond of trust with another if we are not comfortable with ourselves. Issues can easily become confused and communication easily muddled when it is continuously layered with a lack of self-confidence in one or both partners.

For many of us, developing the skills for meaningful communication includes not only being willing to express ourselves but also a genuine effort and interest in listening. There is little that makes us feel as deeply valued and loved as someone taking the time to truly be present and hear us. It is an art that is often overlooked in all of our dealings, but the lack of it is particularly damaging in intimate relationships. Learning to listen actively and respectfully enhances and sustains the life of your relationship.

Trusting your partner enough to share true, central and meaningful aspects of yourself is a true aphrodisiac. It begins a cycle of deepening self-disclosure and safety that is at the heart of thriving relationships.

Consider building a "wind generator" of sorts inside your home, if you are really committed to a sustainable life. Who knows how much energy you might be able to store up for some cold winter night.

Fighting For Your Love

Wyatt wasn't going to come to Bangladesh, and Rachel was seething. She had won a Fulbright—she'd be studying microlending schemes for a year. And Wyatt could be coming too—if they were married. The Fulbright officials had made it very clear that only married couples were eligible for the partner support stipend. They'd been together for six years, and they weren't engaged. What better reason than this?

Wyatt said he wanted to marry her, but not until he was financially stable. And he certainly didn't want to leave his fledgling portrait photography business for a year. Whenever Rachel repeated her plight to sympathetic girlfriends, they only stoked the flames. What was his problem? She could do better, they said. But the truth was that she both loved and was fiercely angry with Wyatt. They could barely broach the subject without Rachel bursting into accusatory tears. He'd been stringing her along. He was afraid of her success, afraid of a third-world country, too focused on his going-nowhere career as a photographer. The fights were ugly and only getting uglier.

And then, mid-fight, Rachel realized what she must have seemed like, eyes wild. She wasn't actually trying to solve the problem—a difference of opinions about a year and a marriage time frame— she actually wanted to hurt him. She wanted to make him feel bad and pathetic and in the wrong so that he'd cave and say yes, and she'd get what she wanted: an engagement ring and a partner for her Fulbright year in Bangladesh. She wanted to make him feel like his business was silly and like he was a spineless loser of a guy. She felt ashamed of herself for the way she was treating him.

She thought of the many geographic sacrifices he'd already made for her, his natural thrift and responsibility and his unwavering response that yes, he did want to marry her someday, but he just didn't feel like this was right. That's when Rachel realized that she had her own issues to work out. If their fights weren't actually about solving a problem, but were just about her desire to inflict guilt and shame on Wyatt, they'd never get anywhere, especially not Bangladesh, and definitely not to their wedding day.

Sometimes you just have to fight. For human animals, conflict is not only a natural outcome of partnerships and family units; it is an essential part of building unity. Our differences may make life more interesting, but learning to deal with them effectively and with love is a challenge for which we are often not well prepared. Learning to speak authentically even if it creates conflict is a basic skill to sustaining relationships. Likewise, developing the insight to see through someone else's eyes, and to have disagreements that build instead of undermine our relationships, requires both courage and a real commitment to stay.

Generally conflicts share similar roots. We fight for power, for freedom, for belonging and sometimes for fun. I was introduced to these categories through my conflict resolution work in the early '90s with elementary and middle school children. While the urge to explore power and deal with issues of exclusion was often fodder for conflicts, I was astonished at how many kids owned up to creating conflict because it was entertaining. Actually, most conflicts are a mix of more than one of these categories; often the reasons are difficult to discern, even for adults. In many long-term adult relationships, these issues morph into the big five classic control issues: around money, family (in-law) relationships, sex, housework and childcare.

Gender issues also affect our reactions to conflict. The male "flight-or-fight" response can create biological changes in moments, and, given free reign, can clash dramatically with the more classic female response to conflict of "tend or befriend." Although there are variations—based on personalities and family histories—It is easy to see how couples might easily fall into the habit of avoiding conflict at all costs. Sadly, they don't realize that the avoidance of the conflict only fuels internal resentment and cuts off any chance for authentic communication. Making more and more room for conflict to live between you only makes more room for real connection.

People hurt other people the most when they're trying to kill their own pain, real or imagined. — Frank J. Page

This quote summed up our early years of marriage, as our arguments were more often intended to hurt the other person than solve a difference. All of the rules you have ever heard about fair fighting should be basic coursework in middle school. Going after the issue and not attacking the other because of your own pain is the mature response to conflict. The other kind only tears down what you spend months or years to build and almost certainly precludes reaching any agreement at all.

Perhaps the most exciting benefit from learning to have the courage to fight with your partner is that honest and fair fights actually fuel your ability to express the fiery passion that makes intimacy sizzle. If you can't disagree safely about day-to-day matters, it is pretty unlikely that either partner will feel safe allowing their more aggressive sexual energies to show. Passionate sex happens between two people who aren't hiding anything.

Besides all that, after 24 years of marriage, I can tell you this: many of those couples that seemed so happy together because they never fought? They aren't together anymore. "Worth fighting for" has taken on a whole new meaning.

Telling the Truth

For months, Lindsay had been carrying on an online affair with a woman she'd known in law school. It had been years since they'd seen each other, and nothing had ever happened physically between them. But there had been chemistry, the kind her relationship with her partner, Elizabeth, had mellowed out of two apartments and a golden retriever ago. Lindsay and Elizabeth were mostly happy together—they argued at times but still found themselves collapsing into laughter in the middle of cooking, or sending text messages that said "I love you" for no other reason.

But Lindsay had reconnected with the woman from law school on a social networking site, and she had begun corresponding with her. It was fun—the desire and flirting satisfied a part of Lindsay that felt like it had been missing since she'd settled down with Liz. Lindsay felt bad, of course, but there was a part of it that she wanted, almost needed. And no one was getting hurt. Liz had no idea, and besides, Lindsay wasn't physically cheating. How could she cheat with a woman who lived in Chicago?

And then the woman came to her town for an environmental law conference. She asked Lindsay to meet for a glass of wine. Lindsay immediately started thinking of things she could tell Liz—she had to go see her trainer, she was meeting with a law colleague. They set a meeting for a wine bar across town. As she was getting ready that night—she'd rushed home from work to take a shower and blow-dry her hair—she realized how much she'd been lying, and how fragile her relationship's foundation of truth felt. The deception of her conversations with this woman was leading toward an inevitable point where she'd really have something to hide.

She also remembered when she'd felt desired and carefree, a woman on her own in the world. That had been a beautiful feeling, and she was enjoying the experience of it again. But there were two people in this relationship, and sometimes it wasn't just about her own personal happiness. In this case, the truth would be sacrificed for something she saw as fun. She heard the door close and Liz walked in with the dog, her face red from the cold. "Where are you going, beautiful?" she asked Lindsay. She knew she had to tell her everything.

Telling the truth in relationships is perhaps the most challenging aspect of relating. Not doing it makes relationships impossible. It is difficult because it takes time to know our own truth and often, even as we get it, truth is as changeable as the days we live in. The wise among us know that there is no truth with a capital "T" and yet there are, without a doubt, lies. That the truth isn't something we can grasp and hold onto makes the work of living with integrity deeply intentional.

We all see things as we are, rather than as they are. We all struggle to find the courage to reveal our own perceptions and feelings in our closest relationships. This is where the world becomes dangerous in relationships. The unexpressed and the lies take up the ground between us. Even if we can't articulate why, we feel ungrounded and fill in the gaps with all kinds of drama and elaborate language to compensate.

We all see things
as we are,
rather than
as **they** are.

Recently I have experienced the weight and reality of this as I watch the demise of the marriage of some close personal friends. It is shocking when the final disclosure of cheating and infidelity comes out; in retrospect, you think you could see it coming for years. During the times we spent with our friends when they were "together," there was always this unspoken space left for the unexpressed—the untruths, and the detachment that grows around them. It was like there was someone else in the room that no one wanted to acknowledge. Sometimes after another glass of wine, the name would spill out of someone's mouth, leaving an awkward silence and a shared recognition of a place too dangerous to tread. Someone would change the subject quickly.

Relationships exist to teach us how to love and to be loved.

I would often leave those gatherings feeling slightly off and wondering what I could have said that would have given the truth some air. I wish now that I could have said something that would have made a difference, but I know that making the commitment to live authentically in my own relationship is work enough. Jamaica Kincaid said, "I am not at all interested in the pursuit of happiness. I am interested in pursuing a truth, and the truth often seems to be not happiness but its opposite."

Although I wish it weren't so, I am coming to believe that sometimes the work of sustaining a relationship that has integrity is not always congruent with my own search for happiness. And yet, on the other side of sharing a relationship that is deeply authentic, there is a satisfaction and comfort to life that surpasses fleeting happiness. When I speak to groups, my first lesson is always to give up the idea that relationships will be or should be easy, or that they exist to make us happy. Relationships exist to teach us how to love and be loved. And while there are moments when relationships feel easy and make us happy, having those feelings is not a reasonable barometer of whether the relationship is working or not.

Sometimes you have to tell your partner something he or she might not want to hear—that you feel lonely, that you've experienced an attraction to someone else, that you need space to sort out your emotions. It takes a deep breath and the commitment to be authentic—to live with integrity—in all of your relationships. Just remember that those feelings are often more about you than about your partner, and own them.

A more honest gauge of whether your relationship is working is the measure of trust and safety that the work of telling the truth builds into it. Because I can tell my husband that "I feel lonely in my marriage" and that he hears it doesn't necessarily fix it, but it does allow me to live it differently. Feeling lonely in my marriage is an honest place. By saying it and feeling it, I have the chance to let it transform. It doesn't mean that it will transform him; it might just need to change me and my relationship to the silence that he is more comfortable living in. Either way, the expression keeps us both honest and in touch with each other and the real struggles that living together entails. In a small and dangerous world, it is truth and love that keep us safe.

You Will Find What You Seek

Erin and her husband, Isaac, moved to Portland, Oregon when he got into law school. Before, they'd lived in Montana where he fly-fished and she mountain-biked and worked as an environmental reporter. She thought that they had a good life, a happy one, and didn't understand why Isaac needed to go back to school. But they made the move anyway, and Erin found herself in a new city with no job, missing her friends and family back in Montana, and missing the mountains and the dry weather as well.

As the months in Portland wore on, Erin became more and more disconnected from life. Job searching seemed pointless and fruitless—the town was overrun with people with just her experience, and she couldn't even get an interview. Everything wrong with her life seemed to point to one place: Isaac. He'd convinced her to move to Portland. He'd started law school, accruing a massive pile of debt that wouldn't allow them to buy a house or take a vacation for years. He was holding her back. The little things he did for her—making her a cup of tea in the evening, watching DVDs in bed—were joyless. Everything was wrong because of him.

She secretly started to apply for jobs in other cities. When she was offered one in Boston, she sat him down and told him she wanted to separate. He'd abandoned her interests for his own, and she was out of patience. Isaac was so shocked he couldn't breathe for a moment. And Erin, witnessing his surprise, realized that she'd never actually talked to him about any of this. It was something her newspaper editors never would have accepted—a one-sided story, a narrative created completely in her head. She hadn't checked with the other party.

Misdirected life force is the activity in the disease process.
— Kabbalah

My husband is a man of very few words, but this is what he said to me when I told him that sometimes I don't know what I am fighting for in my life. Often when I return home from time away, the reentry is full of rebellion. The multiple demands of a complex family life feel like an intrusion, rather than the life that I chose. Sometimes I can slide so deep into the rejection of these demands of marriage and children that the outcome of the story I am envisioning becomes unrecognizable. Spinning an internal story that blames your relationship repeatedly for some unresolved personal issue, or even for the frustrations and transitions that arise from aging, will create a failed relationship.

Our feelings should not be allowed to define our story.

Knowing and naming our feelings is one thing. Like storm clouds that move through overhead, this act cleanses and fertilizes the ground.

But our feelings should not be allowed to define our story. They are too impermanent to carry that kind of weight—and yet this crossover is not uncommon. My own recent forays toward my own identity showed me how quickly my feelings, legitimate as they might be, can spin a story that annihilates the relationships that I have worked for years to build.

You can invent a story that can transform your relationships. Begin with expanding your experience of love in the world. Let the wonder of natural things dominate your senses. Be generous with the love you feel for yourself and others. Smile when you see other people laughing. Watch funny movies or crazy political satire. Invent a story that lets you take nothing small for granted and opens you to the largeness of the present moment. Allow yourself to feel your bad feelings, too—shame, regret, resentment. And then tell your partner how you feel.

Shelter

Brenda was sure that Harry would be angry. Without telling him, she'd signed up to become an essential oils consultant. She'd paid the $200 deposit out of her personal checking account and was now enrolled in a six-week training course. On the way home, she rehearsed her speech: They could use the money, she'd be home to cook dinner every night, this wouldn't affect her time with the kids, as she could do it while they were in school. She wanted to do this. She needed to do this—learning about the oils and their uses, the different herbs and tinctures that went into them, and talking with others about them, she'd felt like herself for the first time in years, since she'd left her job at the pharmacy to stay home with the children. She'd tried to talk with Harry about it many times, but he hadn't seemed especially enthusiastic—just listened and turned back to the paper or said "That sounds nice, honey" and retreated to the back room, where he kept his model railroad and his magazines.

She was home a half hour before him, after picking up the kids from their after-school science class. She spent the half-hour helping them with their homework—but mostly she was distracted and growing ever more agitated as she prepared herself.

"I have to tell you something," she said soon after he walked in the door, taking a breath. And she did.

"That's wonderful," he said. "You've been so excited about this for weeks—I was wondering when you were going to take the plunge. Here, let me show you something."

He walked her to the back room, which was empty, except for a desk and a set of bookshelves. It was painted periwinkle, her favorite color. On the desk he had placed a photo of their family. "Here's your new office."

She was floored—and she couldn't decide whether to hug him or scream at him. So he was listening all along, she thought. It would have been nice to have known that. But then she realized this was no different from Harry's reactions to anything—they were nonexistent. He was always a man of few words. If she needed his input, she'd have to tell him so.

I am not sure if there is a more challenging aspect of relating than communicating. It is the currency of all relationships, personal and professional, and reflects us in the world more deeply than any other part of who we are. Professionally, it is not uncommon for less qualified applicants to get a job over more qualified competitors, based solely on their respective abilities to communicate. Our personal relationships thrive or fall victim to our willingness, and capacity, to self-disclose and listen to the people we love.

The ancient Greek philosopher Epictetus once commented that, "We have two ears and one mouth so that we can listen twice as much as we speak." For all of my work on loving relationships, I have never been a good listener. In my earliest childhood memories, my capacity to articulate and charm almost landed me on TV and kept the peace in my dysfunctional home. I learn about my thoughts by speaking them. Not surprisingly, I married a strong, silent type who makes a living listening to people.

In some ways our very opposite styles of communicating fit. I can attest to the fact that not everyone has the same need to be heard. Yet, I have also learned, often the hard way, that not listening to others with the same attention as you are given guarantees a bumpy road to relating. Even after decades with the same man, I must learn and re-learn how to listen to him. Many times, he has forgiven me for the unconscious ways that I run over him with my fast-paced, fast-thinking articulation, threatening to kill the very thing I have worked so hard to nurture.

Even the best multi-taskers among us cannot truly be listening while doing anything else. My children will attest to the lack of genuine attention they feel while I am half listening in the midst of getting something else done. So many communication errors occur in this half-awake state. We believe that we have communicated when in fact the message has not been sent or, more likely, has been misinterpreted. Or we believe that people know we're listening to them, even when we don't respond to them verbally.

This is largely a result of a thinking error that we all share. Often, we enter into conversations with an agenda, determined and sometimes desperate to have our point of view heard and acknowledged. We rarely go into them with the openheartedness of the explorer.

Curiosity and a genuine desire to understand the person you are talking to changes everything. Creating the uninterrupted space to listen is so close to being loved that in the heart of the one being heard, there is no difference.

This is where our communication, both verbal and non-verbal, is a shelter. Speaking my heart to those who are closest to me, those who always laugh at the right time and want to listen to me until my last sigh, that is the safe haven of my life. We are always communicating—whether it is with what we choose to say or what we hold back. Our eye contact, the way we hold ourselves near others—all of these messages are exchanged continuously. Just as breathing changes by the consciousness we bring to it, adding deliberate and loving intention to what and how we communicate can build shelter in our lives.

Generative Listening

I have been wondering how to listen more and talk less. Anyone who knows me will recognize this as a life quest. Then as life would have it, I was recently presented with another chance to learn how. My seventeen-year-old son has been learning some hard lessons in the gentlest of ways recently, through the eyes of his new girlfriend. Of course, I want to talk to him about it, but recently, as he experienced blinding frustration and fear, I actually just listened. I thought I knew what he would say, but once I stopped thinking and expecting what would come next, I saw him and heard him in a way that is rare between us.

My problem, and one that I share with many, is that I often get stopped at the words, when in fact real listening happens in the spaces beneath the words. Peter Senge describes it eloquently: "You listen not only for what someone knows, but for what he or she is. Ears operate at the speed of sound, which is far slower than the speed of light, which the eyes take in. Generative listening is the art of developing deeper silences in yourself, so you can slow your mind's hearing to your ears' natural speed and hear beneath the words to their meaning."

This kind of listening is a place of grace. It is a mysterious and magnetic force that pulls people into that quiet, attentive presence that allows the speaker and the listener to unfold and know themselves and each other. This is what I think my husband tried to tell me when he said that listening can be a shelter, too. I didn't yet understand the healing and reciprocity that occurs when you absorb another's experience completely. Judgment is replaced; what is left unifies the speaker and the listener so that both people walk away somehow enlarged and expanded.

Often, words don't really describe things nearly as well as they describe our relationship to them. This is where misunderstanding comes from; in our rush to communicate, we often hear the words, but not the heart of what is being said. Slowing down and paying full attention to the people you love gives you the chance to heal and connect in a way that words cannot. I am learning about the power of a loving silence, which gives the people you care about the chance to figure out what is inside of them.

Later that night my son struggled to express his feelings again. Taking the cue I have missed for years, but understood earlier in the day, I simply sat next to him quietly. There he was, finding the courage to look at aspects of relating that I have shouted at him (in motherly directives) for years. Truly no one can tell anyone anything—we must learn it ourselves—but we can be a loving presence to listen and provide what will become a protected and non-judgmental silence.

Listening Inside

For all her life, Molly had known she'd be a lawyer—the first woman in her family to become one. Her husband, Chip, agreed: With her stunningly clear communication skills, sharp mind, and love for research, she'd make a good one. He wasn't even upset when she beat him out for the position of editor of the Law Review. "It's your path," he said. "You were born for this." Even before they were married, they had the future all mapped out: clerkships, partnerships, and then, their own firm. And it was going well. They both earned clerkships, and both worked long hours at their respective corporate law firms.

But everything that had seemed like destiny felt to Molly like penance. If pressed about why she was so tired or seemed depressed, she'd just shrug and say that the long hours were getting to her: It'd all be worth it when she made partner.

It was while doing yoga that she had time to really consider her life. But she was confused. Why, if this is what she was planning for her whole life, wasn't it making her happy? She enjoyed her volunteer work as a Court-Appointed Special Advocate, and the hours she spent doing pro-bono law work for low-income clients in domestic court. There, she felt alive. At least there was that— too bad it was only one day a week, she thought.

Another morning, with her iPod on and the morning's edition of the Wall Street Journal under her arm as she headed into the Y for class, she caught sight of a woman cleaning out the wastebaskets. She recognized her. The woman smiled and waved tentatively, then returned to her work. Molly headed for yoga class. Sometime around the third sun salutation of the morning, she realized she knew where she had seen the woman before. She didn't see her again that morning, but found herself thinking about the woman on her way to work, and on subsequent mornings, looking for her in the hallway. She had been her first pro bono client. Molly knew she couldn't ignore her inner voice any longer.

There is something in every one of you that waits and listens for the sound of the genuine in yourself. — Howard Thurman

Perhaps the most challenging listening that we attempt in this life is learning to listen to ourselves. We know our inner voice well in childhood, but often lose touch with it as the opinions of others dominate our life in adolescence. Sometimes our own still, small voice is replaced by another, more critical one, until we can't hear our own. It is tragic really, how we are trained to not listen to ourselves, to believe that other people know what we want to become or do with our lives more than we do. Listening for this inner voice is sometimes referred to as listening to our instinct, our intuition, or our heart. It may be all those things, but even more importantly, it is the voice of what is genuine in us.

Steve Jobs once said "Your time is limited, so don't waste it living someone else's life. Don't be trapped by dogma, which is living with the results of other people's thinking. Don't let the noise of other people's opinions drown out your own inner voice. And most important, have the courage to follow your heart and intuition. They somehow already know what you truly want to become. Everything else is secondary." The chief dreamer of Apple has clearly lived by his own advice. So why is it so hard for so many of us to listen for and believe what is in us?

In part, our cultural love affair with the mind and all that is knowledge-based is to blame. We trust experts of all kinds about our health, our professional choices, and even our relationships. Our culture is driven by a colossal marketing/media machine that fills our life experience with noise designed to look like instructions for a better life. Many of us never experience silence on a daily basis. In fact a recent study found that the increase in internet social networks has diminished not only time with ourselves but time with our family by more than 30 percent.[16]

Learning to listen to ourselves requires many of the same skills as learning to listen to others. In the same way that we give up our own agenda to hear what is beneath the words someone is sharing, we put aside the incessant thinking that dominates our days. Meditation can help with this: through it, we learn to be fully present, to listen to and observe our own breathing and calm our minds so that we can hear that still, small voice inside us, and to be more fully present.

This is particularly useful when it comes to knowing the truth of our relationships. It is easy to be confused or distracted by feelings of discomfort that are inevitable while in a loving relationship. The intensity that accompanies the sexual dynamics of relationships is often given more weight than it deserves. Often sexuality is a reflection of the deeper listening and connecting that may not be going on in a relationship. And this listening has to start inside.

The skill of inner listening is the only true guide available to any of us. Without it, we can easily fall into a life that does not feel like our own and spend our lives in relationships that don't meet our needs.

Creating the time and space to listen to ourselves is the first step. Even if only for ten minutes a day, sitting with ourselves in relative quiet can be startling. Getting a glimpse of dreams unanswered or grievances unaired may be temporarily disquieting. But following those thoughts and trusting them is a certain route to transforming your life into one of your own making.

Listening with the Body

For women the best aphrodisiacs are words. The G-spot is in the ears. He who looks for it below there is wasting his time.
— Isabel Allende

Recent studies have found high correlations between the music that teens are listening to and the onset of sexual activity. Teens who listen to highly sexualized lyrics were twice as likely to engage in sexual activity than teens who didn't listen to that kind of music.[17] While these kinds of studies can't really explain if the correlation is coincidental or causal, the fact that there is a link leaves us to ponder what kind of listening affects us sexually. How do one's listening skills and habits influence intimacy in all ages of life development?

One of my favorite lines by James Joyce is "Men are governed by lines of intellect, women by curves of emotion." This might explain why most women need to both be heard and to hear loving remarks from their partners in order to turn on their sexual feelings—and why many men simply don't get it. Twenty-five years into our marriage, I am still training my husband around the kinds of comments and endearments that I would like to hear before, during or after sex. But the lack of these is no longer a "deal breaker" for me, because I have realized that his failure to say these things is not a reflection of how he feels about me.

I have often compared the act of making love to a physical conversation. Recently I have been practicing what I have learned about listening in my bedroom as well. The results have been surprising and heartening. Perhaps the most powerful way we can listen to the people we love is not just with our ears and our mind, but with our whole body. The concept of generative listening, which trains us to listen for what is beneath the words, goes to the very core in a physical conversation where messages are communicated with sweeps of fingers, backs relaxing into a caress, a pelvic tilt becoming a shudder.

Our hands can feel vibrations as much as they can other tactile sensations. Let them lead the way into a new kind of listening in your intimate life. The practice of laying on of hands, which has Biblical references to its healing powers, is a simple but powerful technique that can provide real insight into the body. Things inside me literally shift under the steady weight and patient attention of my husband's hands, and he can feel it too. What is more tender than soft hands across a tired forehead or a finger tracing a heart?

If you're not sure how to start this, the Tantric traditions of sexuality are a great place to learn more about whole body listening. For many serious devotees, Tantric techniques are not about mind-blowing pleasure, but about the deep connectedness of souls. Thinking of our lovemaking as another form of listening is, I think, as close as we come to hearing deep into another person's soul.

Our hands can feel vibrations as much as they can other tactile sensations.

CHAPTER 5

Lighting a Fire

Physical love is a mystery of epic proportions. Our most deeply procreative act is also the only human act that has the power to fuse and connect partners so completely that they are transformed. Most of us know that positive sexuality is a powerful glue that keeps the messy aspects of our life cohesive; yet for so many couples, it is one of the most challenging aspects of a relationship to maintain. There are many reasons that positive sexual relationships are so difficult: Good sex is a result of how we think, how we communicate, and how we live together.

The transformative sexuality that we long for requires that touch be safe and secure. If sex has qualities of hiding or worse still, defending oneself, the entire interaction becomes small and narrow and is bound to hurt someone. A couple's ability to explore the world of touch with no expectations and with respect for changing roles provides a basis of confidence in adapting to and working with sexual feelings that may change and grow with your family.

It is said that the person who wants sex the least has the most control in the relationship, but I am not sure that either party feels like they have much control. Issues of initiation and rejection are at the core of many couples' self-esteem and communication battles. One way to change this is to give up the idea that you can or should be "in the mood."

Seriously: The whole concept of the "mood" needs to be eliminated. A good sexual relationship cannot rely on being in the mood. It must rely on commitment to experience loving touch and to offer this touch to our partner. This requires a willingness and desire to be open to your own sexuality. This can be more challenging for women than men, given the changing hormones that surround childbirth, nursing, and growing older. However, the decision to want to find that place is the first decision that has to be made. This took me a long time to figure out, and my relationship suffered because of it.

A lasting and healing sexual life requires a commitment to finding and staying in touch with our own sexuality. Feeling sexy is not something that someone gives us; it is a gift we give ourselves, and the responsibility for it is our own. I often come to my late-night dates with my husband exhausted from my day with four kids and my fledgling business. I know that finding the place inside of me that wants to be touched, and deeper still, penetrated, is a journey.

For men, their sexual drive is external—they can see it and feel it right on the outside of their bodies. For women their sexual drive is internal and deep in their center. I have to give myself permission and sometimes a serious push to want to delve into that place—in part because it requires that I experience my body deeply, in places that I am seldom aware.

Still, I want to acknowledge that even after opening to touch, getting on the road to sexual passion requires a mental leap. There is no other place in life that generates the kind of abandon and wildness that our sexuality does. It requires a letting go of the rational and, to a certain extent, our perceived ability to control outcomes.

There are many good reasons for you to rediscover the passion in your relationship, not the least of which are the benefits to your wellbeing. Scientific studies over the last several years have supported the physical health benefits of a regular sex life. It improves immune functioning, is associated with decreased depression and chronic pain, and even contributes to greater longevity.[18] Equally impressive are the studies that show that people are happier and more satisfied with their overall quality of life when they enjoy a regular sex life. One study measuring self-reported quality of life concluded that the value of a regular sex life would equal $100,000 cash in the bank for people who are not sexually active.[19] I know this works, because whenever we're overdrawn and we have some late night fun, I tell my husband we just deposited another $50,000 into our bank of happiness. We agreed that if we had to choose between love (sexy love) and money, we would pick love.

Fire has always been a strong metaphor for the depth, passion and intensity of physical intimacy. It is nature's energetic equivalent to our sexuality. Fire is the energy of life, providing light, heat and the ability to transform the physical world. Fire in intimacy is the force of attraction that keeps relationships dynamic and whole. Statistically, we are not a nation of fire builders. Couples in the United States struggle profoundly with this piece of their relationship, with over 68 percent of otherwise happily married couples in a recent study reporting problems in their sex life.[20]

Building a fire in your relationship requires first the ground to build it upon. As we discussed in Chapter Two, the ground in a relationship is how you think of each other and your relationship. While there are often moments of frustration or anger in any relationship, if your primary mode of thinking about your partner is negative, then consider the ground. Are you are trying to build a fire on barren land, maybe even in a volcano?

Any fire, once built, requires air to feed it. The air in your relationship exists in the communication between you. The quality and frequency of your conversations and ability to self-disclose is the food for your fire. It is not uncommon for members of a couple to have very divergent interests and ideas. This can actually be a great gift, but not if the result is tuning out and disengaging. How do you listen to your partner? Listening is an act of love that fuels your sex life.

The smallest of fires can become a wildfire without water nearby to keep it in check. The water of a relationship exists in the ebb and flow of the time you share together. Togetherness means different things to different people, and not having a shared definition can make the relationship both unsafe and unsatisfying for all involved.

Good sex then, is both the result and the gift of positive thoughts in your relationship, a steady ebb and flow of together time, and open and honest communication. If the fire in your relationship is not holding, before looking at the problems with the sex itself, look to see if any of these other elements could be improved. I bet you will be amazed at how this affects the fire.

Try this:

Before blaming your relationship problems on your sex life, consider the other elements necessary to build a strong and steady fire.

A Conversation Without Words

For Seth and Kate, physical intimacy and conversation had always come easily. That's what had convinced Kate that their relationship was right, and good. They had met in their early thirties, after each had gotten out of long, failed relationships. By then they both felt whole and complete and with much of themselves to give. They talked for hours – first over cubicle walls at their tech company jobs, when they really shouldn't have been. Then on subway rides and at baseball games, company barbeques and birthday parties. When they'd finally become intimate it was as if a dam had opened: they couldn't keep their hands off each other.

Dates turned into weekends and weekends turned into a brownstone walkup in Brooklyn. Seasons turned to years, and each of them took on new, higher-paying and more stressful jobs. The outpouring of words and touch that had characterized their first years together slowed to a trickle. The usual reasons—stress, expectations that weren't being met—were to blame. Seth realized how difficult it was for him to even consider sitting down and talking to his wife when they were so physically estranged. They needed to have a long talk, not just verbally but physically as well, with tenderness and sex. A lot of what needed to be said—that he still loved her, that he missed the way things were—could be said without a single word.

I have many friends who not only sleep with their husbands only on rare occasions, but are also so distanced from this intimacy that they can't even talk about it. I would go even further and suggest that most of their conversations probably move them further away from intimacy than toward it. Connecting with our verbal language has its limits, especially since men and women don't just speak differently, we also hear differently. This is why I urge all of my closest friends to explore an entirely different dialogue, one where the spoken word is left outside the door and the conversation is led and answered with what some would argue is our true intelligence, the body.

Our bodies do have a profound intelligence, for which we rarely give them credit. Emotions are not actually thoughts running around your brain, although this is how we often describe them; they are actually visceral experiences that live in one's body, as true as chills on a windy night or burning skin under a summer sun.

A conversation without words is often times the only answer in a conjugal life. It took me a very long time to learn this. The countless ways that I would rephrase my frustration with my husband's silences and perceived lack of interest were lost on deaf ears. However, my negative expression and body language were loud enough for him to get my message without needing to hear a word.

Contrary to popular belief, these wordless conversations of the body have nothing to do with being "in the mood." In fact, if you haven't been physically intimate in a while, then the mood concept is moot. A physical conversation requires a willingness to be vulnerable enough to be touched, to allow your body to truly feel someone with you. This has nothing to do with sexual arousal, and yet without this permission, sexual arousal is impossible.

Listening and asking questions with the body are skills we mastered as children. Some of these conversations will culminate in sexual pleasure, while some may provide a physical reflection of the borders that keep you separate. In either case, the journey of opening up to your own body will change the conversation. I guarantee that by taking the conversation to the body you will hear something that words could not communicate. Physical conversations can only help to make the subsequent verbal conversations kinder and more meaningful.

The Initiation Question

It all came down to the question of who wanted it. Sex, instead of a natural expression of love, had become baroque psychological warfare in Gretchen and Ben's marriage, now edging into its second decade. Gretchen, tired from a shift working as an emergency room nurse, would come home, shower, light a candle and try to initiate sex. It was a priority. Ben would sometimes say no, or feel uncomfortable with what she suggested. She had always known she was more comfortable with her sexuality than he was, but this question of initiation was driving small, sharp thoughts into her head: contemptuous thoughts about him, defensive thoughts about herself. They lived side by side in their relationship, but she felt like there was no air or solid ground.

But in their lives the most disconcerting thing was the slack she felt between them in bed. The ground beneath her feet seemed to be giving way. The less they made eye contact in the bedroom, the more they danced around each other like strangers at the breakfast table. It seemed like this question of initiation was exposing a great rift between them. Why had sex become such a destructive tool of power in their relationship? Finally, it seemed clear to Gretchen that something had to give, or their marriage was going to fall apart. They had to rebuild the fire.

This topic is a bit of a Pandora's Box, but I am going to try to simplify it a bit. Sexual desire, or the lack thereof, is the result of a complex range of internal experiences that includes everything from hormonal stimulation to a prehistoric form of communication. Our ability to feel sexual is at least partly influenced by the culture and family we live in. Between couples, it is deeply affected by the communication that forms the basis of the relationship.

As stated earlier, these complex issues often boil down to arguments about who initiates sex and what response the initiator receives. The classic "I am not in the mood" or "I am tired" responses create a cycle of defensive and offensive reactions that is almost like a pre-patterned dance. It's a scenario that many couples just don't have the vocabulary to navigate.

Two things transpired in my marriage to ease this issue and allow us to experience sexual desire without the burden of fear and unmet longing.

Little snarky comments break down the fabric of trust and take a long time to mend. So to begin: promise to not say anything mean to each other. That doesn't mean you won't have negative thoughts—just don't share them in a negative or mean way.

For me, making this safety agreement made a huge difference in my self-esteem and also my relationship. The issues around initiating lost their power as we both began to feel safer and more loved. That Christmas, my husband also gave me lingerie for the first time—a gift-wrapped invitation to explore my sexuality without the pressure of the old dance. The more we laughed and explored the new space, the more the old space disappeared by itself.

There are still times when one of us might not feel in the mood when the other does, but now it doesn't mean anything more than what it is—bad timing.

Here are a few great ideas for shifting the initiator discussion so that you can enjoy the moment:

Number One: Offer to love someone with no expectations. Love oil massages of the back, feet, and neck can ease tension not just in the body, but between each other.

Number Two: Agree to just kiss for a few moments. Love oil is good here, too. Or, better yet, suspend the moment just before the lips touch and feel how close you can be without touching.

Number Three: Try a new venue. If you are always inside, go outside and hug. Try a chair instead of a bed to cuddle on. Hold hands while eating dinner, even if you're only having leftovers at the kitchen table.

Feeling wanted sexually carries so many meanings and has a great deal of emotional baggage attached—a lot of it unspoken even to ourselves. The weight of these unspoken messages can start to feel like there is an invisible third person at the party. Shame of rejection is not a lot easier to bear than the shame of chronic lack of desire. We all know this story in some form, and we continue to analyze it, trying to determine responsibility: Placing blame seems like the easiest way to live with the pain of unrequited desire.

The first thing that helps to stop this cycle is to identify it. Find a neutral time to bring up the topic with your partner. Agree that you will look at the issue from a distance, almost as if you were talking about people you both know. This can be difficult to do, especially if the conversation is overdue. The moment you can both see the patterns that your intimacy falls into, there is a peace that comes from not being alone with it. This doesn't solve the problem, but it allows you to create a new relationship to it—one of witness and investigator rolled into one. It makes you take the time to learn to separate your feelings from the event.

Promise
to not say
anything
mean
to each other.

Once you have both seen the issue from both sides, you can slowly unpack your feelings and start to explore what it means to you and to your partner to be sexually desired and to feel sexual desire. It is really important to keep these discussions in the present tense. Don't be tempted to justify your behavior and feelings, because that will remove the possibility of healing the moment. Keep in mind that by healing the present moment, you automatically heal the past.

This is not a quick-fix solution, and it doesn't alleviate the push/pull of living in a relationship, but by working to eliminate the sting and pain of rejection, abandonment and whatever else has been attached to these swings, you allow yourself the joy of exploring them.

My husband and I now pass the weight of relating and intimacy back and forth on a squeaky but functional pulley that we have both come to understand and appreciate. It's a relief to have the freedom to invite an interlude without the fear that saying no will start another battle. Allowing yourself and your partner this freedom is a gift that will repay you many times over as you discover the joy and spontaneity of taking turns.

Penetration

Penetration is the word often used to describe the culminating act of sex. It's a word I often use when describing the best use of a good lubricant. But recently, after using the word in conjunction with the act, I wondered what I was saying. The verb "to penetrate" has six different definitions in the dictionary, and as with any metaphor, the meaning one attaches to the term may deeply influence our relationship to the act.

The act of **penetration** is a **force of nature** that is **loaded with meaning** and **mystery.**

A friend of mine once told me that it is not uncommon for many of her lesbian friends to maintain a no-penetration relationship, and among my heterosexual friends, it is not a small minority who avoid penetration with their spouses. I never asked them, but I wonder if for them, the meaning of penetration feels like the definition of a military force entering into enemy territory or the depth of a projectile into a target. Certainly the idea of women as targets for men is pervasive, and so the need to protect oneself is also deeply held.

To penetrate also means to have an effect throughout, to spread through; permeate, move deeply, or imbue. Applied again as a metaphor for sexuality, this penetration is an act that transforms, that has the potential of changing everything. This sexual act can have the force of inspiration, the possibility of being completely saturated with love.

The act of penetration is a force of nature that is loaded with meaning and mystery. Not surprisingly, to penetrate also means "to gain insight and to have a marked effect on the mind and emotions." Our language about our sexuality is as layered as the act itself, and knowing what you mean when you speak about love and sex can only be helpful.

Sexuality is a metaphor for many things in life. Those things that we share in our sexual encounters, like language, attitudes and openness with one another, have a long reach into the depth and closeness of our day-to-day relationships.

Consider your relationship to penetration—the word, the idea and the act. Penetration means all of these things all at once. But if I were to make a leap, in the name of making love sustainable, it would be that couples who build a strong and consensual relationship with the meaning and act of penetration are much more likely to have a strong and consensual relationship to each other.

Making Time for Love

Josie and Phil barely saw each other. Especially in bed: Phil worked during the night shift at a lumberyard and Josie worked during the day as an HR manager. Sometimes they even passed each other in the doorway with a kiss on the lips, and then headed in separate directions. Their sex life had always been happy—they'd only emerged from their honeymoon suite for meals—and they had kept a passionate connection as their marriage had mellowed into its second decade. Josie had always prided herself, secretly, on their spontaneity—the time they'd torn each others' clothes off in a rowboat on a secluded lake, the time they had furtively fooled around like teenagers in a parked car in their own driveway, just feet away from their bedroom but unwilling to wait. But the truth was, their new work schedules were taking their toll. In the moments that did find them in bed at the same time, Phil was usually exhausted. Josie's flirtatious advances seemed to go unnoticed.

She started to look at herself longer in the mirror, wondering if something had started to go and if Phil could tell and didn't want her anymore. Weren't men supposed to be the ones full of libido, all the time? It was definitely driving a wedge between them, especially as Josie decided to pretend as if their sex life didn't exist and wait for him to seduce her. That didn't happen, and the hurt went deeper. Finally, she decided to start asking him on "dates"—dates that would set them up for a sexual encounter. He was thrilled, and sent her e-mails and phone messages inquiring about the night's date. Spontaneity, she decided, was for people with time on their hands. Good sex in a busy life took planning.

Making time for love is an important indicator of the commitment and sustainability of your relationship. When you consider the outrageous scheduling hoops we agree to in our work settings (or even more intensely, in managing our children's activity calendars), it makes you wonder how the idea of scheduling intimacy could still be so taboo.

Yet, taboo it is—many of us seem to have an overriding belief that sex and intimacy are somehow tainted if they are not spontaneous and immediate. This belief system is connected to the shame and guilt we carry around from our adolescence (when we could only describe a make out session if we could first say, "I don't know how it happened, but suddenly we were just ..."). It seems we can only fully embrace our sexuality if it just happens to us. Planning for it forces us to claim the most unpredictable, and to some degree, uncontrollable, aspect of our life.

There are a lot of good reasons to start including love time in your regular schedule. Leaving love to the spontaneous in a life that is overbooked with commitments to family and careers means that love often gets the lowest ebb of our energy. Most of us arrive at our bedrooms exhausted, finally turning away from the last email, the last bill to be paid, the last dish to be washed, the last light turned off. Even the most spontaneous among us can barely muster the energy to imagine a wild interlude at that moment.

Planning love dates can add excitement to the rest of the week. Looking forward to an intimate time, which can but doesn't have to include full-on sex, can be both relaxing and stimulating. Couples who are struggling to find physical connection may find it easier agreeing to mutual massages than envisioning hours of lovemaking. Either way, setting aside time and energy for your partner sends a message that sustains commitments. While my husband and I don't have set days of the week, we do discuss and agree to "dates" either later in the day or the next day. Setting this time for lovemaking becomes part of the foreplay and gives us permission to entertain thoughts that might come in handy later.

Inventing a shared language for intimacy also connects partners. Revisiting the art of flirting can spice up even the most common of conversations: "What's for dinner?" suddenly has multiple meanings. We are more playful with each other when we are waiting for our date time.

Learning to schedule time for love requires that we acknowledge and are willing to talk about our sex life together. This is challenging, because the taboo is so strong against speaking honestly and openly about sex. Yet developing a language for love is one of the strongest predictors of having a good sex life. Couples who can talk about what they want or prefer in their physical lives may actually be able to get it. Code words are okay—they may even add some excitement to the game. As long as you make time to play.

Try this:

Give up the idea of being "in the mood" or feeling emotionally satisfied as the impetus for intimate contact. Think of it, instead, as a health resource. There is no other physical act at our disposal that carries the physical, emotional and spiritual benefits of making love with someone you love.

Habits of Love

Mike had the heart attack at a time when his marriage seemed to be ebbing. He and Diana had been together for 26 years, and by this time their sex life could best be described as "cursory." While they had a beautiful Craftsman home on a quiet lane, two grown children in various stages of higher education, and an exemplary vegetable garden, their relationship was stagnant. They talked about the dishes and the car insurance, decided when to visit their daughters, and dealt with the minutiae of their shared life. But they had long since stopped revealing anything deeper than the superficial. They were roommates who slept ten inches apart in the same bed. They co-existed—living in the same house, walking the same Golden Retriever, attending some of the same dinners and work events. But that was all.

The sickness came from inside, from his heart. One night, he was doddering around the kitchen, work shirt untucked, hair mussed, fixing an evening snack, while Diana read in the bedroom. He fell hard and Diana heard him. If he had passed out onto the soft couch, she never would have thought to get up or wondered where he was or what he was doing, so separate were their orbits. Diana, the wife he had once thought of as his one true love and his soul mate but now considered mostly as his roommate, rushed him to the hospital. He had an emergency triple-bypass as she wept in the waiting room. She felt wracked with guilt: she knew that she had allowed herself to become just as numb as he was, complicit in the daily routine of distance and disinterest that had calcified to become a wall between them. She had wasted so much time.

After he returned home, they set about bringing him back. Somewhere in the midst of his naps, his new, low-cholesterol diet, and his slow return to his feet, they both realized something: They were more than bored roommates. They loved each other— actually, they needed each other. This love, in fact, was really the only thing that would keep them healthy and happy. They could not take each other's presence for granted any longer.

As the days passed, they began to disclose more, healing the
wounds of the past several years. Sometimes it was painful.
Each realized how little you could know or understand about
someone you had been living with for 26 years. But they now
knew that their very well-being demanded that they work at loving
each other. As they rebuilt his body and their relationship, they
promised to be engaged again—not as they had been as 22-year-
olds, with a diamond ring and a horizon stretching ahead of them,
but engaged in a more meaningful way: as people who were not
just co-existing, but who were committed to loving and really
living together in the world.

> Love and intimacy are at the root of what makes us sick
> and what makes us well, what causes sadness and what brings
> happiness, what makes us suffer and what leads to healing...I
> am not aware of any other factor in medicine—not diet, not
> smoking, not exercise, not stress, not genetics, not drugs,
> not surgery—that has a greater impact on our quality of life,
> incidence of illness and premature death from all causes.
> — Dr. Dean Ornish

These words began a revolution of thinking about the critical
connections between our physical well-being and our level of
connection in life. As a heart doctor, Ornish paved the way in
demonstrating that not only a mind/body connection, but a heart
connection, determines our well-being, our ability to heal, our
most basic ability to enjoy life. In some ways, these scientific
studies only underline what we have always known: Love is the
cure as well as the illness in our world, and evolving our ability to
love increases not only our chances of survival but creates a depth
and meaning in life that only happens in relationships.

The healing effects of intimacy and connection extend deeply into
the physical act of lovemaking. Hundreds of major medical studies
have shown that an active sex life leads to a longer life, better
heart health, a healthier immune response, reduction in chronic
pain symptoms, lower rates of depression, and even protection
against some cancers. Men who have regular sex (even twice per

week) have half as many heart attacks as men who only have sex once per month. In fact, a regular garden-variety sex life has been shown to extend life by as much as ten years. People who enjoy a meaningful sex life are less anxious, fearful and inhibited.[21]

All the habits that you develop about sustaining your environment and home can also apply to your relationships. Feed your relationship with the same energy that you bring to the selection and preparation of your food. Giving your time to composting and recycling is no different from finding the space to air out your feelings. Making commitments to simplify your life and reduce your impact on the environment requires the same amount of mental energy as constructing the space and time for deep and meaningful touch in your days.

People who enjoy a meaningful sex life are less anxious, fearful and inhibited.

And just look at the sustainability benefits: Not only will you be happier and more optimistic as you take on the challenges of dealing with our quickly changing biosphere, but you will likely be healthier and have more time to make a real difference.

Game of Love

Rachel had a game she liked to play with her husband, Tom. It wasn't a fun, sexy game they played in the bedroom. It was a martyr's game. He'd come home from work rumpled and tired, ready to withdraw into his world of books. But Nancy had other ideas. Surely he knew that their son had a trumpet performance tonight, and that such things were the currency of marriage, of family? No, apparently not. When he demurred, she assented, digging the car keys into her palm.

"Go ahead, stay home, I know you're tired," she'd say through gritted teeth. "I'll go to the trumpet performance. You've had a hard week."

The second she slammed the door of the van, she'd be silently fuming, adding up a precise list of all the times she had given him a pass, and another list of how many times he'd stepped up. These days, their relationship had all the playfulness and joy of a trip to the dentist.

They were always trying to outdo each other in some way, to show who was the better, more dedicated spouse and parent—and who was the flaky, undeserving slacker. Rachel would lie in bed at night while her husband slept and tally these things, building a case for prosecution in her mind while she watched him snore.

But something funny happened. Rachel never actually won anything. For all her stoicism and sacrifice, Tom never magically became exactly what she wanted to be. He was still just Tom, who missed trumpet performances and never brought home flowers, but who, when she took the time to notice, volunteered to walk the dog in the rain and helped their daughter build a seven-story model space station for science class. Just Tom, the same guy she'd married 11 years earlier.

She never gained the upper hand—and if she had, what would that mean, anyway? She thought about it and decided that maybe really loving someone wasn't about winning or losing. She decided she needed to relearn her game: Maybe, as the kids' soccer coaches preached at every practice, it wasn't about who won or lost. It was about how she embraced the process of loving someone.

It is said that love is everyone's favorite game, and yet even with all the new technologies designed to help us connect, more and more people are opting out—preferring to live alone, rather than to risk another bad relationship outcome. This preference reflects a deep change in our collective human psyche, for it used to be that what lovers feared most was loneliness. Now, being caught in a static or unsatisfying relationship is even more troubling. Wanting to be together, to build a family, is no longer enough.

I have spoken with several people who have expressed this sentiment. When I pressed the point and asked them: If they were to meet a compatible, kind, and intelligent partner, would they truly feel like there wasn't room in their life to accommodate them? There was a brief pause, and typically some variation of "I'm not sure" was as close as they would come to an answer. Our modern age has made it easier to be passionate and to maintain that passion about a pet or a favorite sports team than a lover. What has happened to the game of love?

Memories of childhood games on late summer evenings remind me of what the game of love once meant to us. As kids we understood that it was the play that mattered. Winning and losing reflected their original meanings, which were "to desire" and "to be set free," respectively. Playing capture the flag or a full neighborhood game of hide and seek in the dwindling light was an apprenticeship in freedom. Pretending was rich with excitement, as we all shared in the wonder of not knowing the outcome. And yet we all knew that no victory was ever final—there was always tomorrow night.

Lovers in the past shared one secret. They knew that it wasn't about winning or losing, it was the play that was essential. Playing allows us to experience freedom from duty and necessity. It is a primary condition of creativity and allows us the unselfconscious delight of living out alternative realities. It is what makes us so deeply human.

Nowhere does this ring more true than in our most intimate moments. Adding playfulness to sexual desire invites new friends into the bedroom: imagination and fantasy. Invite these allies to any passionate encounter with an openness to play, a willingness to pretend, and the freedom to live in the wonder of not knowing the outcome. Saying yes to this game of love keeps life fresh; while it offers no guarantees of long-term winning, it does promise to share glimpses of what we all desire most.

Playing this game doesn't guarantee a life without bruises or the happily-ever-after story that we all long for. It will, however, teach you about all the many ways you can love, and love again.

Is It Ever Too Much?

When Julia read the newspaper article about a couple who'd taken on the project of having sex each and every day to kick start their marriage, she immediately felt tired. With a two-year-old and a six-year-old at home and a demanding job as a public defender, she could barely stay awake long enough to brush her teeth. Sex had become a rare occurrence in her marriage, and she sensed that her husband, Thomas, was just as tired as she was—he barely even tried to initiate lovemaking any more.

Not surprisingly, Julia and Thomas had become more and more estranged from each other as the focus had shifted from themselves to what seemed like a daily struggle just make sure everyone made it to work, daycare, or school fully clothed and fed. But that night, after the kids were finally asleep, as her husband sat upright in bed staring with glazed eyes at the 11 o'clock news, she mentioned the newspaper article. He laughed.

But then they looked at each other, with the same "what the hell" look that had led them to get married by an Elvis impersonator in Las Vegas nine years earlier (followed by a bashful phone call to each of their families, and, six months later, by a wedding at a country club). So they tried it. And it was good. And then the next and the next and the next day – despite their exhaustion, they worked it into their nightly routines, just like brushing teeth or watching television. The sex, and their connection, heated up like they were newlyweds. Now when they slogged through a day consumed by work, commuting, parenting and home chores, they knew they had something to look forward to—not evade, or even dread—in bed at the end of the night. Too much was never enough.

If you have ever wondered what happened to your active sex life, or can't even remember what it feels like to have a sex life, then the books *Just Do It*[22] and *365 Nights*[23] will either inspire or depress you. In each, a couple takes up the challenge to refresh their marriage with a daily dose of sexual intimacy.

Successfully combining an active and satisfying sex life with a married lifestyle is the subject of volumes of books and a frequent focus of my own writing. It is epic to achieve the same with kids in tow (and worth noting that neither of these couples have any, which in my opinion makes their achievements noble, but not quite heroic).

The truth is that
intimacy
begets
intimacy.

With or without children, the authors of the *Study of American Sexual Behavior* note a "strong relationship between rating your marriage as happy and frequency of intercourse."[24]

"What is harder to say is what the causal relationship between the two is," they note. "We don't know whether people who are happy in their marriage have sex more, or whether people who have sex more become happy in their marriages, or a combination of the two."[25]

The truth is that intimacy begets intimacy. Sexual intimacy creates a singular connection that paves the way for better communication, emotional closeness, and physical release that is unparalleled in any other activity that we share. The converse is true as well: couples who communicate well and show up for each other regularly are more apt to be drawn together physically. The experiences of the couples in both of these books both bear this out: Their experiments did bring them closer together in every way and also gave them the space to develop a broader and more comfortable language for sex. This, not surprisingly, improved their sex lives, even after their respective experiments ended.

Frequency of sex is not really the point, however. As the authors will attest, people's needs and capacity for sexual intimacy vary. Sustaining the emotional space that leaves you feeling interested and safe enough to be vulnerable and open to great sex is, in and of itself, a remarkable kind of intimacy to live in.

There have been times when my marriage has experienced a "dry spell" of physical intimacy, most recently last summer, when poison oak and crazy schedules took over our lives for a while. The tension and stress between us wore more deeply, and the lack of physical closeness turned the edges of all our encounters brittle.

The longer the dry spell, the more challenging it is to open up in the ways that bring our physical intimacy into daily view. So here's an experiment: See what happens when you make time for intimacy three days in a row. One day at a time.

Try this:

Commit to some form of physical intimacy every night for one week, and watch what happens in your relationship.

First, Love Yourself

Masturbation was a dirty word. That's what Iris had been taught—at home, in school, and by the world at large. It was a dirty, shameful thing that would make you the object of ridicule if anybody found out about it. Iris had barely touched herself in private, and now her husband was asking her to do it. After having prostate cancer and surgery, he'd lost some sexual function, and they struggled to find ways to connect intimately. He'd asked her if she'd be willing, and she immediately blanched. She had never really masturbated alone—and he wanted her to do it in front of him? It was too great a leap.

Iris loved her husband and wanted to do what she could for their marriage. But the possibility of finding her own pleasure seemed remote. Iris, home alone one Sunday afternoon, tried touching herself, and found that her first response was shame when it felt good. But wait—it felt good, she, Iris, felt good. So she kept going, reminding herself that she was home alone.

Stripping away the anxiety and shame attached to masturbation was slow and difficult. Her husband stopped bringing it up, but she realized that she needed to do this not just for him, but for herself. As Iris explored her body, she grew to feel less like it was silly, or ugly, or embarrassing to understand the secret places within her. And someday, when she felt right, she'd share it with her husband. But for now, the process was about exploring Iris. She had to love herself first.

Certainly masturbation is a topic that could do with a little airing out. It wasn't all that long ago that boys were tortured with all kinds of strange contraptions to stop them from experiencing the "terrible" act of masturbation that was sure to make them blind or insane. Hard to believe, but the most educated people around perpetrated these myths—often under the guise of medicine or religion—for years.

Ironically, women with "hysteria" were also medically treated by being masturbated by the physicians who eventually built elaborate room-sized vibrators to take over the handwork of bringing women to orgasm.[26]

Back in 1995, Good Vibrations, the San Francisco-based retailer "trusted for more than three decades to provide a comfortable, safe environment for finding sex-positive products and educational materials to enhance one's sex life and promote healthy attitudes about sex," launched National Masturbation Month to protest the firing of Clinton-appointed U.S. Surgeon General Dr. Joycelyn Elders. Conservative members of the administration blasted Elders when she responded to questions regarding safe sex by saying that "Masturbation is something that perhaps should be taught."[22] Getting over our discomfort with masturbation and healthy sexuality is not only important for ourselves, but for the next generation. Opening the dialogue with the young people in your life and normalizing the language of sexuality is one of the most important steps you can take to build sexual health into your family's future.

But cultural myths die hard, and physical self-love still carries a heavy dose of guilt, shame, and anxiety for many people. As I have been researching the topic, I can tell you it only takes saying the word out loud to silence a crowd.

Feeling isolated and alone with our sexuality seems to be a standard theme in this country. The sex education that is provided through adolescence is at best an exercise in naming body parts, and in some institutions is more like a diatribe of abstinence theory and the sinfulness of sexuality in general. Some historians have suggested that "the forbidden fruit" that is referenced in the story of Adam and Eve n the Bible is the experience of orgasm, so it is not surprising that this first gate of knowing and loving ourselves through masturbation has been rejected by certain religions as sinful.

If you have ever watched a small child explore his or her own body and the witnessed look of happy surprise when they discover the highly innervated erogenous zones that have no other purpose than pleasurable sensation, it is clear that the shame and discomfort that often replaces this healthy curiosity is a result of our collective education. We are all subjected to it on some level.

We are all sexual beings. The degree to which we are driven by this part of our human nature is as variable as is the way each of us interprets and acts on it. I would like to suggest that we rethink and embrace the idea and practice of healthy self-pleasuring.

Finding comfort with our sexual selves is one of the most genuine, intimate and life-affirming ways we can know ourselves.

Finding comfort with our sexual selves is one of the most genuine, intimate and life-affirming ways we can know ourselves. It is the first gate of understanding for both the raw experience of pleasure and our primary sexual identity, which is a prerequisite to a fulfilling sexual relationship with others.

Just for the record, masturbation, although a taboo subject, is the most common sexual practice on the planet. And it's not just for lonely people, either. Survey research shows that people of all ages masturbate, both in and out of relationships. Kinsey's survey found that almost 40 percent of men and 30 percent of women in relationships masturbated.[28] A study of *Playboy* readers found that 72 percent of married men masturbated,[29] and a study of *Redbook* readers found that 68 percent of married women masturbated.[30] Despite these statistics, many people feel the need to hide this behavior from their partners.

Theory to Practice

Physics is to mathematics as sex is to masturbation.
— Richard Feynman

Learning how to love is a complex set of equations. Knowing
how to love is no more an inborn skill than being able to do
algebra, although for many of us, algebra will prove to be less
challenging. Physical loving turns these basic math facts into the
complex calculations that are the glue of the physical universe.
Seen in this light, masturbation is like learning our basic math
facts. Our physical and sexual anatomy is at once universal and
individual. Gaining an understanding of our own sexual organs
and discovering reliable pathways to pleasure is a prerequisite for
any possibility of a shared enjoyment.

Your
orgasm
is your own.

Sigmund Freud once said "The only thing about masturbation to
be ashamed of is doing it badly." Indeed masturbation is one of
the healthiest behaviors we can add to life. It can help to keep
our genitourinary tracts healthy into old age, and it teaches us to
become and remain responsive sexual partners. Learning how to
experience pleasure alone can have a meaningful positive impact
on a number of sexual problems between couples.[31]

One of the best reasons to let go of all the judgment and history
surrounding this normal sexual behavior is that having access to
your own pleasure and orgasm teaches a profound inner lesson:
Your orgasm is your own. No one else gives it to you or has power

over you having it. Having the knowledge of what feels good to you allows you to share that most intimate information about yourself with someone else. Accepting full responsibility for our own sexual natures, needs, and preferences is the gift we can bring to a healthy sexual relationship with someone else.

So take the time to love yourself. Feel your body and be grateful for all the sensations that you experience.

Try this:

Spend some time alone getting to know your body. Touch yourself without shame or guilt, and discover what feels good to you.

Pain and Pleasure

Sex had always been a reliable way for Erica to find pleasure. Daily runs and dancing had given her a body that she felt at home in. Even her work was that of the body. When she'd met Kyle in graduate school for physical therapy, their connection was palpable and visceral. They began a physical relationship where the sex was uninhibited, joyful—almost an extension of the basketball they played together or the hikes they took.

As the years went on, they took trips to Costa Rica to hike through jungles and kayak underneath waterfalls. They felt as if their lives were in sync: during they day they each went off to heal bodies, and at night returned home to each other. But what Erica knew, and what gnawed a little under the surface, was that there were vast, gaping silences between them. But those silences were easy to fill with the pure physical pleasure of sex or exercise. During those times, she felt herself connect with Kyle.

They were married, and soon Erica was pregnant. The pregnancy was difficult: she threw up for months straight, while Kyle continued to drive off with his kayak atop the truck and head into the mountains. After their daughter (who they named after a favorite river) was born, Erica avoided sex. She'd had tearing during the birth, and her post-pregnancy body was strange and unfamiliar to her.

The sex hurt, and the reliable physicality that had sustained the core of their relationship was hurting too. How would she and Kyle relate to each other? What would cement their relationship while she tried to understand her body again? The line between pleasure and pain was so close.

There is a "pain and pleasure" principle that informs sexual desire and romance as well. It is an indescribable, yet palpable reality of sexual intimacy, wherein the ecstatic release of deep pleasure balances and ignites an equal experience of pain. Every time I have sex, I try to understand the relationship between these forces that seem to live at my very center. The experience is so profound, it feels at the time like an almost life-changing event; even with my partner of more than twenty years I struggle to find a language to describe the sensations without feeling like I am crossing a line into pornographic exposition.

We have in fact discussed how challenging it is to find language to explore our intimate relationship and how awkward and inadequate much of the language feels. Part of the problem is that so much of the language has been used and abused by the pornographic industry that it is hard for us to feel comfortable in the same milieu. Still, once we move beyond the shared discomfort of our limited vocabulary, the discussion about the lines between pain and pleasure are worth exploring.

The relationship between pain and pleasure in human sexuality is as profound as it is complex. I have long wondered what begets what, if it is actually the intensity of the pain that arouses the pleasure or the other way around. The French have long called orgasm *le petit mort*, or "little death." Orgasmic release exists in a place that is solely its own; I know I am not alone in identifying it as both pain and pleasure.

Love, sex, pain and violence all stimulate the release of similar chemicals and hormones in the human body. Endorphins that are released in painful experiences are often felt as pleasurable.

So it is not surprising that the practice of combining painful techniques with sexuality is ancient. Roman poets, ancient tribal drawings and even the Kama Sutra all refer to safe practices of what has become known as BDSM, or Bondage, Domination, Sadism and Masochism.

The medical analysis of BDSM is as checkered as the practice itself. It has been thought of as both disease and mental illness through most of the development of psychiatric practice and even dating back to the early 1800s. Although these kinds of sexual practices were taken out of the diagnostic mental health codes in the mid-1990s, there are still many people who struggle with their own relationship to the desire to explore and experience pain with sex.[32]

Studies in both the US and Europe have estimated that the overall percentage of BDSM-related sexual behavior in the general population ranges somewhere between 5 and 25 percent depending on sexual orientation, age and location of the study subjects.

There is a subculture of BDSM practitioners throughout the world, and clubs or "dungeons" are established in most large cities in the world. BDSM practitioners make an important distinction between their sexual choices and sexual abuse, as everyone involved must agree to be safe, sane and consensual. This includes the use of "safe words" and other boundaries of consent and safety.

The connection of pain/pleasure has existed for most of recorded humanity; there are many people for whom this form of sexual behavior exclusively defines sexuality.

Feeling like our sexual arousal mechanism and desires are normal can be a big concern for most of us. Finding a language to talk about your sexuality and desire is not always easy, but it is the first step to meeting your physical desires and creating the emotional intimacy that makes sex meaningful.

Here's my hypothesis: Loving someone emotionally creates the same pain/pleasure experience that physically making love to them does. There are moments of deep connection and intimacy, vulnerability and nakedness. And with them comes an open door to the opposite experience: feeling deeply hurt by your lover by what was said, or, just as often, what went unsaid.

The act of loving—in whatever form—requires a willingness to experience both the pain and pleasure. This is the piece of sustaining loving relationships that is easy to miss, or at least misunderstand.

Tantra for the Uninitiated

Simon and Emily were busy people. They lived in San Francisco were at exciting points in their respective careers: Their lives were a series of work trips, networking dinners, and endless hours at their respective law offices. They had worked hard for their condo, with its Brazilian cherry wood floors and view of the marina. They were both competitive, and the same forces that propelled them through the ranks of their law firms also tended to give them an active and aggressive sex life. Neither had a problem reaching orgasm.

But when they had sex, Emily (and Simon) each ran their own separate race, each with both eyes on their own separate orgasmic prize. More and more, their lives felt mechanical: the nice home, the hard work, the handsome couple attending events, the sex that was a robust, but almost robotic, release. Then Emily lost her job, and suddenly everything seemed a lot more fragile. The disconnection between them could no longer be covered up with constant activity—Emily needed Simon, and she didn't feel like they saw eye to eye anymore. In fact, they barely looked at each other.

After reading an article about Tantric sex, she suggested they try it. He thought it sounded interesting and kind of titillating. No longer could they make love in their own separate worlds of pleasure. Their bodies, and more than that, had to work in unison, picking up subtle hints. They found themselves locking eyes, something they had never done before during sex. Suddenly running the race alone didn't seem so appealing.

Centuries old, Tantric practices are part of a much larger Hindu/Vedic tradition of which sexuality is only part. Tantra is a lifelong spiritual quest that demonstrates the interconnectedness of everything and includes yoga, meditation, and breath work as well as sexual techniques. The Western and more modern interpretation of Tantra has become synonymous with spiritual and sacred sexuality. Tantric books and practices explore and teach techniques that are capable of elevating the participants to a sublime and ecstatic spiritual plane.

Many teachers caution against the confusion associated with "tantric bliss" as a path to intense orgasmic pleasure. In fact, the power of the practices is often the sublimation of orgasmic pleasure toward a rising spiritual energy of divine connection.

There are dozens of books and videos along with more than 500,000 references listed in a Google search about "Tantric Sex."

I am not an expert or even a devoted student of Tantric practices. Yet there are a few simple techniques that I often recommend to customers and clients without even situating them in the context of Tantra, which in fact is where they came from.

Step One: Keep your eyes open. The idea of making love with your eyes open is one of the fundamentals of deep connection in intimacy. It is surprisingly harder to do than you might expect. Move toward this idea as an intention, rather than a rule; you will be amazed as the collection of glimpses will reshape how you think about your partner and yourself. It is not easy to be seen, even by the people we love. Truly witnessing the act of love is profoundly transformative.

Step Two: Mind your breathing. Becoming conscious about your breath is central to all yogic practices and is foundational in Tantra. An easy way to begin this is to intentionally count your breaths together and to find a rhythm and timing that you both share. Slowing down with each other and taking a breath with each connection is incredibly exciting.

Combine these two ideas into one of my favorite intimate activities, one that I believe is worth repeating. As described earlier, see if you can get to the finish line together. Again, keep looking into each other's eyes, and distinguish between deep and shallow penetration. Start with shallow and move toward deep penetration in a rhythm that you both follow. This will require concentration and focus, which alone changes the nature of intimacy. The first round is nine shallow and one deep stroke, each one connected through breath and eye contact. The second round is eight shallow, two deep. The pattern continues and then repeats, if you can.

Have fun.

Imbuing our physical love with intent and attention is the key to transforming love into a force of unity. My first line of products was called Sacred Moments. Even without any formal study of Tantra, I sensed that the closest we can get to the divine is in the act of making love to someone you really love. Have fun.

Sexual Healing

Olivia and Adam had been married for six years. For two of those years, Adam had been having an affair with a yoga teacher, a colleague of Olivia's. He had ended it and confessed to Olivia, but the trauma had very nearly ended their marriage.

Adam had convinced her to seek relationship counseling together. Aside from the broken trust that now clouded every shared act of their life together, she felt a stunning sense of sexual rejection. She now lived with the knowledge that her husband had actively chosen another woman to share the most intimate experience with, and for her it cheapened all the times that they'd lay in rumpled sheets together, too.

Months later, their marriage seemed to be slowly recovering. But Olivia, much as she felt she had forgiven Adam, couldn't bring herself to sleep with him—at least in the way that she had before. Any openness and sexual abandon that she'd once had was now brittle and dried out. Even her body, usually blessed with natural lubricant and easily orgasmic, ceased to respond. Though she was a yoga teacher, the concept of mind-body balance hadn't become fully real until this point. Forgiveness was one thing, but sexual forgiveness was another. And until she could deal with the dark, wordless pain that went with a feeling of sexual rejection, until she could understand that, she couldn't begin to truly forgive her husband.

Sexual healing is only possible through forgiveness. The injuries and betrayals that we sustain as we negotiate this most mysterious human interaction are as diverse as life itself. How these injuries embed themselves in our identities defines our sexual relationships, sometimes for life. While this is also true for other emotional injuries we sustain, the pain associated with sexual encounters is deeper by definition; it encodes itself on us viscerally. Because sexual education is almost non-existent and sexual topics often taboo, many of us have very limited language to express our sexual experiences, good or bad.

There are times when talking provides nothing. The words are all inadequate to the experience; it is through the tenderness of touch that injuries can be felt and released. This is human alchemy, impossible to describe even after you have experienced it—it is even more impossible to instruct someone else in finding this path. The ancient quote by Roman emperor Marcus Aurelius provides a hint into this process: "The sexual embrace can only be compared with music and with prayer."

Among its profound mysteries is the power of intimacy to heal; often it is enough to move forward with the right intention and an open heart.

These are the most fragile and tender of exchanges that we humans are capable of sharing, and it is easy, even with the best of intentions, to hold too strongly, to let go too soon, to not feel the other person's response in a timely and sensitive way. To err is human and oh, how human we are. Yet to forgive is the only way to stay together.

There are times when sexual trauma is too much to handle by yourself. Counseling is never a bad idea, and in certain instances is essential to healing. The American Association of Sexuality Educators, Counselors, and Therapists offers an online referral service on its website, www.aasect.org.

Fantastic Imaginings

> A central agent of the erotic act, of eroticism, is the imagination…if that goes away, that's when the breakdown of desire often occurs. — Esther Perel, *Mating in Captivity.*

I often tell people that the sexiest part of their body is their brain. Usually I am trying to help them recognize the connection between their olfactory system and the limbic part of the brain where memory, emotion and sexuality are activated. But the more I talk about it, the more I have come to realize that this is also a key entry point to our sexual imagination and our capacity for fantasy. We all have our own personal brand of eroticism—how sexuality is transformed by our imagination—but we don't all have equal access to it.

By definition, long-term relationships provide a safety and stability that many of us crave. However, taken too far, the attachment to safety can also diminish the erotic vitality of the relationship. When we close our relationship to the element of surprise, we suffocate what is mysterious, raw and evocative. Suffering with bad or mediocre sex often has a lot to do with choosing safety over the mystery and separateness that makes living together vital. This is where having the capacity and courage to access our imaginations in our sexuality can reinvigorate our relationships and our intimate lives.

Applying your imagination to sexuality is more than just the cliché ideas that come to mind for many people when they hear the word "fantasy," such as costumes, props, and scripts for sale in adult stores. Allowing your imagination free reign during your lovemaking times allows you to "experience things that you can't possibly act out," wrote Alex Comfort, M.D., in the classic bestseller *The Joy of Sex.*

"Fantasies can be heterosexual, homosexual, incestuous, tender, wild, or bloodthirsty—don't block, and don't be afraid of your partner's fantasy; this is a dream you are in."[34] Trust and intimacy bloom when partners risk sharing their most private thoughts with each other.

That said, there are many thoughts that dance through my mind during sexual intimacy that I wouldn't repeat even to myself. I know I am not alone in this, as Nancy Friday's bestsellers *My Secret Garden, Forbidden Flowers* and *Women on Top: How Real Life Has Changed Women's Sexual Fantasies* all demonstrate. Start by allowing your fantasies to spark passion in your lovemaking. As your intimacy warms up, so will your ability to share with your partner.

In fact, some of the fantasies that you never thought you could tell anyone about actually occur to most of us. A poll of 10,000 people conducted by *Men's Health* magazine in 2010 found that both men and women share the same five fantasies.[35] They include: Self pleasuring while partner watches, experimenting with a variety of domination and submission roles, having sex in public (think elevator, or back row of an airplane), making a pornographic video, and inviting a third person to bed.

The first steps to living out a fantasy with your partner can be as small as buying a pair of soft fuzzy handcuffs for the privacy of your own bedroom or experimenting with the dining room table in a new way. Sometimes seemingly small changes in routine are all it takes for us to wake up and actually see the person we are loving. Taking your fantasies to a new level takes the courage of first bearing witness to them, being able to communicate them, and then making clear agreements (with even clearer boundaries) about the new explorations. You'll take a risk, but the reward is an intimate life that only you can imagine.

Biology of Affairs

> We always deceive ourselves twice about the people we love—
> first to their advantage, then to their disadvantage.
> — Albert Camus

Most people who have affairs will say that they don't know how it happened. Extramarital affairs are rarely consciously planned; they happen, as life often does, with one thing leading to another. Evolutionary psychologists, in attempts to understand infidelity, have found some interesting patterns that suggest that our biology might again be the leader in our life choices.

Depending on the study cited, between 30 to 60 percent of all married couples in the U.S. are impacted by infidelity.[36] More interesting than the differing rates of occurrence for men and women are the different patterns of infidelity for each gender. Cheating men are more likely than cheating women to have an affair with someone younger than their spouse. On the other hand, cheating women are more likely than cheating men to have an affair with someone better educated than their spouse.[37]

...between
30 to 60 percent
of all married couples
in the
U.S. are
impacted
by infidelity.

Additionally, marked sex differences exist in age patterns of infidelity. Women are far more likely to commit infidelity in their twenties and early in their relationship, whereas men's affairs happen later in their relationship and predominantly after the age of forty. Evolutionists believe that this pattern reflects a long-term mating strategy and that, just like other mammals, our biological clock and often unconscious drive to reproduce may be exactly what is happening that inspires infidelity.[38]

The biological changes that impact sexuality with aging and menopause are additional aspects that underlie infidelity. I have watched many of my closest friends both leave and be left during this intense life transition. Is anyone to blame, when fully fifty percent of women lose their interest in sex or struggle with arousal and orgasm right when a man's need for sexual satisfaction and validation is at its most vulnerable?[39]

Yet our sexually driven biology is only one part of the human story. While sex and love are inextricably linked, the processing of these experiences happens in different regions of the brain, and while there is some overlap, it is the experience of love that matures the mind. The constellation of neural systems and activity involved in the experience of love strengthens with the length of the attachment. As a recent study concluded, "Romantic love is one of the most powerful human experiences…more powerful than the sex drive."[40]

Although some might question the veracity of these claims, try to remember how potent the experience of falling in love was for you, extending far beyond the sexual, to the very core of what it was to be alive. Loving over time does change your brain. Although it doesn't often have the intensity and ecstasy associated with "falling in love," it carries even more benefits in terms of long-term happiness and health. When you are feeling your biology influence your choices, make sure you also consider what makes us truly human—our drive to love.

CHAPTER 6

The Mysterious O

Most people have an extremely limited language to work with when it comes to orgasm. This collective silence about the mystery of orgasm and how it affects our well-being and our relationships impacts a stunning percentage of the population. Many studies, including a 2001 study of sexual behavior with more than 27,000 participants from 30 countries, have revealed that orgasmic dysfunction is more the norm than the exception.[41] One third of all women have never experienced orgasm; a second third experience orgasm only rarely. Orgasmic dysfunction is not just a woman's story, however; equal numbers of men suffer from a range of issues that hinder their ability to experience orgasm.[42]

The word orgasm is derived from the Greek word *orga*, meaning explosion. This makes sense: The experience of orgasm often feels like a burst of pleasure, bliss, emotional and physical release. In fact, the moment of orgasm creates such a complete letting go that the brain center that controls anxiety and fear is switched off.

Orgasms are as unique as each individual who experiences them. The wide variety of intensity, location and stimuli that contribute to and create orgasm plays a big part of the mystery that many women experience in identifying what an orgasm "feels like." Interestingly, studies have found that the confusion about experiencing orgasm goes both ways: Some women claim to have had an orgasm yet show no bodily response, while other women who do have classic response like vaginal contractions and heart racing believe that nothing has happened. The modern mythology (and, dare I say it, pornography) of orgasm looms so large that many of us are not even sure how to identify our own.

The good news is this: The more orgasms you have, the more orgasms you're likely to have in the future. Learning about your own sexual response and developing your orgasmic potential will bring both immediate gratification and long-term satisfaction. As with any skill-based human motor function, all bodies come equipped with the tools for orgasm, yet without proper education and opportunity to practice, many people never successfully achieve the synergy of mind, body and spirit to release this unique and revelatory experience. It is a quest worthy of our time and attention.

The first step on this journey is taking the conversation about sensation, pleasure, and orgasm out of the adult entertainment industry and into the privacy of our bedrooms. This may seem like stating the obvious, but, actually, intimate sexual conversations are more rare than you might think. This is a tall order, given the combined impact of the lack of sexual knowledge we're raised with, our shared cultural anxiety, and how little scientific knowledge is available about sexual response.

Orgasm is the human expression of life force. Whether you are among the lucky few who know it as the height of intimate relationships or are among the many who seek to know it better, it is a currency that affects us all. Everyone wants to orgasm.

Of all the coveted human experiences, what makes orgasm so elusive is that it cannot be forced. Many methods of cajoling even seem to backfire. Desperation and orgasm are strange bedfellows. Here we only need to unleash our imagination for a moment and it is clear how much sexual behavior lives in this odd coupling—faking, purchasing, role playing, submitting, dominating—what we will do for an orgasm is somewhat astounding. Several great sex therapists I know tell me that the quest can cost many people their relationship. When it is the relationship itself that provides fertile ground to grow and nurture our comfort with our sexuality—that is what opens the door to orgasm.

It isn't that surprising then, that statistically, your chances of having an orgasm are much better on your own than with a partner. Letting go of your judgments about sexuality—yours and that of others—is easier to do for many people than digging deep into the fears and insecurities that most of us carry about our sexual history, preferences and behaviors (not to mention our bodies). Many people spend their lives married to people with whom they can't even say the word "masturbate," let alone imagine sharing the act.

Everyone wants to orgasm.

Being able to orgasm with someone, or for that matter by yourself, requires safety. It is the most exciting letting go available to us. Where could we be more vulnerable than in the ecstatic release of one's center? Being able to find a language to explore the kinds of touch that are stimulating, allowing the strange fantasies that lurk in all of us to be revealed, and letting your body lead you into feelings that you don't and can't control are all essential to experiencing orgasm that transforms.

It doesn't work to focus on orgasm as the finish line. Aiming for it makes the journey anxiety-ridden and makes you forget that you are on a journey. Often times it is the smallest of details that can push you to a place that you didn't know was in you. But you can't feel that place if you are looking for something big ahead of you. Presence is nothing if not the key to our sexual selves.

There are probably as many different types of orgasms as there are people who experience them. For me, orgasm is a journey that always brings me back to my center.

Getting There

Having an orgasm starts with feeling aroused. No arousal, no orgasm. Arousal begins in the brain, specifically the limbic area of the brain where our sense of smell intersects with our emotional process, our memory, and our sexuality. Vibrations of arousal and eventually orgasm live in the body and are triggered in the brain.

Arousal
is expressed
through our
breathing.

Trust your sense of smell and indulge yourself with whatever scents awaken your sensuality. Napoleon was well known for requesting that his wife abstain from washing for a week when he was coming home; for other people, a certain cologne is the ultimate in sexy smells. Whatever works for you, remember that our olfactory system has always been foundational to the art of mating—and use it to your advantage.

Arousal is a visceral experience, and bodies are built for motion. Nowhere is this more useful than in sexual exploration. Although this may seem like stating the obvious, it is not a small percentage of people who tense up and stop moving around in their sexual activity. There is more than hip thrusting with which to experiment: Moving all of your limbs, rolling your neck and stretching into new positions can trigger arousal points that you didn't know you had. If you can think of no other reason than wanting to understand more about your orgasmic potential, try to fit in a bit of core strengthening exercises (such as Pilates or yoga) into your life. Being able to hold onto someone you love from the inside will make you feel both strong and sexy.

Arousal is expressed through our breathing. Whether you tend toward long and slow breaths or short, fast inhalations, stop and notice how your breathing affects your connection to your body, your lover and your orgasmic possibilities. Try changing your breathing pattern and see how it transforms the experience. Synchronizing your breathing and movement with that of your partner is a remarkably simple technique that has profound impact on lovemaking.

Extending the space between arousal and orgasm is the art of lovemaking. Do your own solo experiments, so you know the sensations and buildup that lead you to the point of no return. Practice pulling back from that line and introducing another form of touch or breathing, and then move toward it again. I have long been an advocate of waiting as long as you can to surrender to your orgasm. The longer you wait, the more power and energy is built up and the sweeter the release. Some spiritual techniques suggest moving up and down this arousal tunnel, coming close as possible to your orgasmic edge without going over, as a spiritual practice. Sounds like a worthy form of meditation, and I don't question its incredibly powerful results.

Arousal messages come through our body as genital secretions. As many as a third of all women do not have a strong natural lubricating response.[43] This easily turns into feelings of low libido and disinterest in sex. After years of birthing and nursing babies, I never have natural wetness, so I was heartened to discover that a small application of great, clean lubricant will kick-start the arousal cycle as well as I remember natural lubrication did. Not only that, but adding healthy lubricants ensures painless friction, more time to experiment and a more likely orgasm.

Fantasy can either be helpful or harmful in your orgasmic journey. Having fantasies that conjure up guilt and take you out of your physical experience and away from your partner are generally not going to move you closer to orgasm. However, healthy fantasy can be seriously passion producing. I can never repeat the strange and fantastical thoughts that go through my head, but as I have come to bear witness to them, I have experienced whole new levels in my orgasmic potential.

So go forth and flirt with arousal.

So go forth and flirt with arousal. Don't judge your experience or compare it to anyone else's, and enjoy the ride. If there is any journey worth taking over and over again, it is the one to our most innate and miraculous human pleasure.

Setting the Stage

A lot of things happened in Peter and Abby's bedroom. Work happened: It was a home office with a computer, fax machine and jumbled papers spread over desk and floor. Entertainment happened: the television was used for movies and cooking shows. But one thing that happened very little was sex. Surrounded by the evidence of their chaotic lives, the couple usually collapsed into an unmade bed, sweeping off clothes, books, cell phones and papers.

Abby realized one day that the last time she'd had an orgasm— quite some time before—she had been in a motel room, of all places, on a weekend trip. She remembered the slightly illicit delight she and Peter had felt when they'd dropped their suitcases on the ground and closed the door behind them. A bed, unfamiliar and unfettered with household debris. A quiet room with nothing to do but...have sex.

That had been a long time ago, Abby thought. Looking around the bedroom-office-closet-den, she wondered what would happen to their sex life if the bedroom became a place that felt less like an extension of the daily grind and more like a boudoir. It wasn't just the actual comforter and mess on the floor, it was the way they thought of the bedroom. It wasn't a sacred space; it was just like the rest of their busy lives. So one weekend when Peter was out of town, Abby revamped the bedroom. Out went the television and the office equipment. It was superficial stuff, really, but the bedroom already felt different. The new sheets and banished TV were one thing, but the effort and the acknowledgment that sex was a priority was something else. Peter came home from his business trip, and she followed him up to the bedroom. He loosened his tie, dropped his suitcase on the floor and together they repeated the best part of what had happened at the motel.

Your bedroom should be the place where you sigh deeply and your whole body relaxes. The bedroom is your nest, a singular space that both regenerates you on a cellular level every night as you sleep and provides the environment and impetus for physical intimacy. As the place where we love deeply, procreate, and regenerate ourselves, our bedroom is our sanctuary.

I know there are many late-night TV lovers who will argue the point here, but I still say that a television in the bedroom is one voice too many, especially if you are in a committed relationship that is fragmented by the busyness of life. Same goes for newspapers and news magazines. Watch and read in the living room, the kitchen, or the bathroom if you must, but leave the bedroom to the wonder of silence and soft voices. The older I get, the more convinced I am that life must provide a retreat or we wither on the vine. There are numerous sleep studies that back me up on this: Screens and sleep are incompatible (and screens are definitely of little help in jump-starting an intimate life).

So don't let the world into your nest. Guard the sanctity of the space. Set the stage for love.

Try this:

Make your bedroom a sanctuary for love. Invest as much attention and energy in your love space as you would to set your table for company. Easy additions such as candles, cozy bed pillows and throws can create a retreat. Consider excluding digital distractions such as a TV, phones, and laptops that make it easy to avoid intimacy.

Spark It Up

Many people do not know how to have sex. On the one side, we are inundated by an exhibitionist, "anything goes" sexuality in our pornography-laden culture; on the other side, there is nothing—an empty and lonely place where most of us live with our questions about sexuality, wondering what is "normal." Even most "Better Sex" videos are so graphic that integrating the images into practice is a far reach. I sell products that I guarantee will provide the tools for a longer and more satisfying sex life, but the longer I do it, the more I recognize that even the best lube in the world is not going to work if you don't know how to use it.

So here's a little guide to the steps of making a spark turn into flame in your bedroom.

Step one: Desire Arousal, Arouse Desire

Desire does not always precede arousal. Sometimes if you give yourself a chance to explore the purely physical sensations of scent and touch, the body will open up by itself to desire. Many a night, we have a pre-set agreement for an intimate rendezvous, and I arrive exhausted, with no desire in sight. This is where love oil comes in. Scent is experienced by the olfactory and registers in the limbic part of the brain, where memory, emotion and sexuality are waiting to be stirred.

Discovering desire is about waking up arousal; it is striking the match that lights the fire. For me it feels like a process of falling deep into my body, a journey that awakens feelings of a thousand tiny fireworks just under the skin. Each and every time I take this journey of arousal, I realize again how cut off I am from really feeling my body through most of my day. Good sex should always begin with this journey, where the goal is learning to feel everything.

Step two: Exploring Fantasy

The body is now awake, so whether you and your partner have private fantasies that you would never repeat, enjoy visual candy in the form of books or video, or actually plan and try on roles together, go for it: Healthy sexuality lets us abandon our normal reasoning selves and give way to our passion.

Whether orgasm is easy or challenging to achieve has a lot to do with your ability to let go and experience the odd and fascinating part of being a sexual human. Experiencing the pleasure of intimate touch without any fear of being somehow abnormal (which perhaps most people fear about their sexual selves at some point) is how you move toward orgasm. You can't demand it; you can only make room for it.

This is the place to experiment, to see how different tactile surfaces and vibrations change and enhance your experiences. This is where the flame builds.

Step three: Penetration and Lubrication

I never pull out the lubricant until I can't stand it anymore, until I can't wait another minute. It wouldn't do its job in step one or step two; it wasn't made for those places. Accepting anyone into you as deeply as intercourse allows is a sacred and life-changing moment. Lubrication eases the entry and creates a dynamic smooth gliding of tissue against tissue. There is nothing more explosive and deeply satisfying than sharing the fireworks of deep intimacy and the connection of our most private selves.

Intimate Mindfulness

> The most precious gift we can offer others is our presence. When mindfulness embraces those we love, they will bloom like flowers. — Thich Nhat Hanh

Canadian sexologist Lori Brotto[44] has applied the ancient Buddhist principle and contemporary healing modality of mindfulness to sexual dysfunction with heartening results. "We spend far too much time worrying about whether we're 'normal' or good enough," says Brotto. "Mindfulness is about cutting out that kind of noise and tapping into what your body is doing." Her research shows that many sexual dysfunction symptoms aren't generally caused by physiological wiring problems, but more often by a psychological mind-body disconnect.

Applying the practice of mindfulness to our intimate experiences is healing, not only because we commit ourselves to being fully present, but because we do so with non-judgmental eyes and a gentle heart. Often, the disconnect we have with our libidos comes as a result of the over-thinking that our unspoken sexual insecurities and fears create.

It doesn't really matter what kind of anxiety you bring to the bedroom; as soon as the mind starts spinning, you leave the present moment and it becomes impossible to focus on the sensations in your body. Thoughts of work, family concerns or body issues literally take you away from the visceral experience of contact. This is where the mind turns off the feelings in your body. Forget about arousal: You might not even feel someone pinch you when you are lost in your mind.

A good way to begin to quiet the mind and bring yourself into the moment is to rely on the senses. Sensuality is really nothing more than connecting to your senses deeply. It is in the smallest of sensations that this practice comes alive. For instance, actually feel the different textures of skin on your partner's body, or feel the weight of his or her hands on your lower abdomen, run your fingers through his hair, trace her face with your lips.

It was waking up to the power of scent that first deeply shifted my ability to be fully present in my own intimacy. Being consumed by your sense of smell with someone you love carries the intrinsic power of presence.

Mindfulness takes practice. Incorporating some silent times alone where you can learn to notice and watch your mind at work is a good foundation for the practice in the bedroom. Letting go of erroneous thoughts on your own will help when you get distracted with a partner. Learning to stay focused on the sensations you experience with your partner can be more challenging than it sounds. This is why mindfulness is often associated with loving kindness. Mindfulness has a snowball effect in life—helping you be more present not just in your lovemaking, but in everything else.

What better place to begin to practice it than with the person you love? Showing up mindfully and experiencing the remarkable range of sensations that physical love and arousal creates in the body will transform your relationship and your life.

Yet even when sparks are flying, your partner might not know exactly what you want. Try a few of these subtle yet clarifying ideas to communicate your desires and preferences without feeling like you are giving orders or interrupting the flow.

1. Make it a game. The popular childhood game, Hot and Cold, is a great way to playfully direct your mate to the places that you most enjoy being touched. Any time you turn your communication into a game, you build up suspense and anticipation. For example, if your partner is kissing your neck and you say, "you're getting warmer," you might be pleasantly surprised by the many unexplored erogenous zones your partner discovers on his or her way to your preferred spot. Playfulness and laughter are the prelude to passion.

2. Use fantasy to your advantage. I can always pique my husband's curiosity when I start any conversation with "I had this fantasy about us, and you were doing _____with me." Opening up your lover's imagination both lets him know that you are thinking about him in sexy ways and gives him/her permission to try new things. Sharing fantasies is a playful and effective way to move your love life into new territory.

3. Let someone else do the talking. Both men's and women's magazines offer monthly advice for improving your love life. Sometimes giving someone a good idea can be as simple as leaving the magazine open to the right page on your bed. If that doesn't work, a simple conversation starter like, " I just read this interesting, crazy, cool (pick your adjective) article in this magazine. What do you think about....?" Books and television shows can also be used like this, so look for good sources to get your conversation started.

4. Show rather than tell. One of the most effective forms of correction in many activities is by noticing and using the teachable moment. When his or her hand isn't quite placed correctly or if the pressure is too soft or hard, lay your hand on top of your partner's and show her how you like it. Experiential learning not only lasts longer but also often translates into other areas of relating.

5. Compliment instead of complain. Your sensitivity to your partner's ego in sexual performance is well founded. Most of us have a raw nerve about being able to pleasure the people we love. Rephrasing what isn't working into a statement of what would make your experience hotter is easy to hear and listen to. Try "I love it when you... And it would be even better if you..." Instead of complaining about what is or isn't happening, you are channeling current behavior into sexy new possibilities.

Extending Life and Love

Teresa hadn't had an orgasm in a long while. But this was not something her husband Al realized, because Teresa was a prolific faker of orgasms. It had started one sweaty night when Teresa was too distracted and tense to give in to Al's sincere sexual ministrations. Teresa, who was the type of girl who ended up running all the charity committees, organizing every bake sale and chaperoning every field trip while doing the job of three people on one person's salary at work, wanted to please people, and she always had. She was popular and well loved. She was also terrified to disappoint.

And so on this sweaty night in Teresa's bedroom, she decided to tell a little white lie and fake an orgasm. She felt so comfortable and good with her husband, she didn't want to disappoint or discourage his efforts. She just wasn't getting there tonight. So she channeled Meg Ryan in "When Harry Met Sally" and let loose with a few moans. It worked—Al was happy, and a few moments later, snoring peacefully, leaving Teresa awake and tense as ever. The orgasm faking became frequent, and eventually her default mode. Al was clueless. Teresa realized that the lies—she prided herself on her honesty and candor with her husband in every other aspect of their lives together—were driving something surprisingly large between them.

She began to resent his own pleasure in their sex life, and the way he seemed so happy and content that she was climaxing. It's really just good acting, she thought bitterly. But more importantly, why was she doing this? And how could she stop? She realized that she felt so tense in the bedroom that unwinding and getting to the core of her complicated sexuality would take a lot of time and tenderness. And she just didn't want to burden Al with that responsibility. But at the same time the woman who wanted to please everyone was not being pleased herself, and she knew the situation was untenable.

She had to come clean, even if it meant the risk of hurting Al, if she was ever going to live in a genuine sexual union. So one night as they slipped into bed, she confessed. Instead of being angry or hurt, Al listened. And suggested they just take it slow tonight, see what happened—no pressure. And that night she didn't climax. But it was wonderful in other ways, and she felt a little of the tension disappear. And days later, when she did have one of those earth-rearranging orgasms that seem to reverberate into the sky, it was something she and Al really experienced together. Something real.

Having regular orgasms will extend your life and provide the basis for a long-lasting relationship. Recent studies have confirmed the link between longevity and frequency of orgasm.[45] We know that people who enjoy a regular, satisfying sex life (i.e. regular orgasms) are less stressed, less depressed and generally in better physical, mental and emotional health.

Here are some things we know about sex in relationships: The swing between feeling desirable and connected in a relationship is in continuous flux and reflects the health of the entire relationship, not just its sexual side.

One of the most common blocks to a shared orgasmic experience is the strangely common practice of faking orgasm. Studies cite as many as 60 percent of women have faked an orgasm; this practice is not limited only to women.[46] The reasons for faking orgasm are complex. Whether it is because you feel like you can't perform, or that you can't open up to that level of vulnerability, or that by faking you feel like you can end the intimacy, what results is the most serious of breaches in trust. Faking orgasm is a lie, and it leads the person who is trying to love you and bring you pleasure to feeling like he or she cannot trust the messages they are hearing. Breaching trust at such a naked level of vulnerability cannot help but seep into the other aspects of the relationship.

Many women mistakenly believe that their own pleasure doesn't matter, or they don't want to burden their partner in their frustrating search for that mysterious and powerful orgasmic release. But real conversation about these issues is sexy. It communicates that you are invested and trust your partner enough to be vulnerable about this most deeply held desire. Just for the record, most men get more pleasure and sense of mastery from helping a woman they love to orgasm than their own climax.[47]

Working together to find the path to individual orgasm is the most intimate sharing that exists. It changes everything in a relationship.

Finding a language to talk about sexuality is, for most people, the stumbling block. As in any other area of personal development, clarity is everything. Learn to talk about *your* sexuality.

Take the time to think about or write down your own personal sexual history, including orgasmic experience. Share these notes with your partner; often even unwilling partners will begin to open up. Set a couple of shared goals: Mysterious as our sexual selves may be, they respond to dialogue as well as any other part of our life. For many couples, making efforts to de-stress their lives can have remarkable effects on their ability to be intimate.

Learn to talk about *your* sexuality.

Discovering pleasure together is like pouring the concrete for your relationship's foundation. Knowing that you have the ability to reach someone in this most intimate of ways is one of the most significant sources of self-esteem that relationships afford. While sharing orgasm is not enough to keep a relationship alive, the inability to move toward it is enough to kill it.

Positively Sexy

Portia and her husband, Alex, had been married for two years. She sometimes felt unaccountably lucky: From the storm of her tumultuous youth and meandering early adulthood, she had stumbled upon Alex in a small town where she was practicing as a legal aid lawyer. He was a social worker who helped one of her clients.

Portia was proud of their marriage—opening up to Alex and letting him past the stern, driven, pantsuit-wearing lawyer she had worked so hard to turn herself into felt like a major feat. But there was one place where Portia couldn't open up. She had never had an orgasm, and while the sex was frequent and apparently pleasurable for Alex, even thinking about connecting on that level made her profoundly uncomfortable. Deep inside her where an orgasm should have been lived a kernel of an idea that sex and pleasure were bad, and that if she ever let go—really let go—she'd never get herself back. She wondered if her 1970s Kansas sex education classes had taught her that, or her parents' threats that she should never have sex before marriage or risk being seen as a slut. Whatever it was, it was in there. Deep.

Evening after evening, Portia found herself standing naked in the bathroom, staring at her body after they had finished making love. She felt such shame and guilt attached to her softening body. She loved her husband, felt tied to him over bagels in the morning and while walking their dogs at night. But she wondered if she would ever be able to truly think of sex as anything other than a marital duty, and her body as capable and worthy of experiencing orgasm. But she wanted to. On more than one night, she squinted at the mirror and surveyed her own body, and she thought about how far she'd come from a small town in Kansas to a job and life she loved in another city. Over time, the guilt and shame she'd attached to sex started to fall away. Finally she turned her back to the mirror and walked into the place where she could start to change her mind about sex—the bedroom.

"Sex-positive," a term that's coming into cultural awareness, isn't a dippy love-child celebration of Orgone—it's a simple, yet radical, affirmation that we each grow our own passions on a different medium, that instead of having two or three or even half a dozen sexual orientations, we should be thinking in terms of millions. — Dr. Carol Queen[48]

Imagine if we believed that we all had a basic right to sexual health. Instead of shame and fear-based explanations of sexuality, which mostly focus on avoiding sexuality, what if we were all privileged to a comprehensive sexual education that was both non-judgmental and focused on the life-enhancing aspects of human sexuality. Imagine if we grew up believing that pleasure was a normal and healthy part of maturing sexuality. The world could not stay the same.

The term sex-positive has been floating around since the early '80. This idea tried to make a space for respecting and creating healthy sexual identities and relationships. Working to redefine a culture that makes us fearful and ignorant about sexuality—our own and that of others—is a process of education and intent. It means going beyond the limited view of "normal" and recognizing our sexual prejudices for what they are, much as one would work toward an awareness of racism, disability-phobia, or other forms of systemic prejudice that influence our judgments and our actions.

Many companies have adopted the term sex-positive to differentiate themselves and emphasize their belief in providing products, education and resources to create a healthy sexual society for everyone. In addition to paying attention to the quality of their products, they also normalize the huge range of interests and identity that make up our collective sexuality.

Embracing our Sexual Selves

"Sex is something you do, sexuality is something you are." These words by Anna Freud help us move beyond the compartmentalizing of our sexual selves. Establishing healthy boundaries around our sexuality is different from the prisons we build for ourselves by continuously denying our sexual longings and feeling ashamed about our sexual identities. Unlocking the door between who we are and what we choose for our sex lives is fundamental to building a life that includes intimate pleasure.

Take the opportunity to re-educate yourself about what healthy sexuality means to you and decide what you want your children to know about their own sexual development. Build a curriculum for yourself and the people that you love that allows you to expand your ideas about your sexuality and experience pleasure without shame. We are sexual beings, and this instinctive procreative urge has the power to transform all aspects of our health.

Try this:

Create a library of reliable sexual resources that can educate you, open your horizons to intriguing new possibilities, or ignite a flagging libido. Bookmark a few reliable and entertaining websites that speak to your sexual sensibilities. Cultivate relationships, professional or otherwise, where you have a safe haven to explore your sexual questions. Choose to do the work of growing a sensuous life.

Develop your Sexual Vocabulary

Until we can talk about our sexuality and fully embrace it, we don't stand a chance of having the sexual relationship we desire. But there are many barriers to doing so. Many people have trouble talking about sexual topics, including me. Even with all the work and writing about sex that I do, I still find myself in awkward and uncomfortable situations where I am unsure what words to use, how much to share or explain, and even whether it is my place to be the one explaining.

Usually I break through my discomfort, sometimes placing my foot squarely in my mouth, because I believe that even more important than knowing the right words is the intention to break the silence that weighs so heavily on our sexuality. This is an ironic statement when you consider how much exhibitionist, titillating sexual talk fills the internet and even mainstream media. Yet when it comes to discussions about improving intimate lives or even sharing sexual health information with the next generation, we are all silenced. Thinking about how to recognize and overcome some of the following obstacles might help you develop an ease and a vocabulary for having meaningful sexual conversations in your relationship.

Sex Myths: The biggest sex myth, in my opinion, is that in order to be great lovers, we should all be mind readers. The idea that you should simply know what will turn on your partner does a great disservice to many a relationship. Communication isn't always about talking, but learning to feel comfortable with anatomically correct language is worth the effort. For most of us, communicating is much easier than learning to read minds.

Sexual Fear: Many people walk around with fear associated with sexuality. A common fear on the list is not being "normal," which makes many people keep their desires secret. Another is the fear of sexual rejection, and/or making a fool of oneself. Considering how naked, literally and figuratively, our sexual lives leave us, these fears are understandable, yet also clearly not helpful. Hiding our sexual selves or feeling ashamed cuts us off from ourselves and makes communicating nearly impossible.

Negative Beliefs about Sex: Many of us were raised with some negative sex beliefs. For some of us these are very personal like bad feelings about your body (ugly, dirty, fat, etc.) or the more universal and religion-based sanctions against sexual pleasure. Whichever is your flavor, all these beliefs are poor openers for a good sexual conversation.

Lack of Information: To be able to discuss sexual issues and concerns, it helps to know the basics. Unfortunately, many of us never benefited from any real sex education. Lacking accurate and basic knowledge of sexual organs and how they function makes a real conversation difficult. Not knowing the reasons you feel or don't feel something can make the topic all the more frightening and exacerbate our fears and negative beliefs often without our awareness.

Privacy and Boundaries: Sexuality is one of the areas that we hold most privately in our life, especially as we get older. People's sense of privacy and propriety even impacts their ability to buy products in a grocery store. We all want to have good sex lives, but we don't want anyone else to know about it. Creating the privacy you need to feel comfortable about your sexuality should actually enhance your ability to communicate about it. But using the lack of privacy as an excuse to avoid the conversations will not get you closer to what you want. Having a clear sense of your personal boundaries is essential, because sharing your sexual questions and issues will require you to be vulnerable in ways that are uncomfortable. Finding your own comfort zone might take crossing the line a few times, but feeling confident in your ability to stretch within your boundaries will help build your ability to communicate.

Learn to Walk the Talk

Learning the language is only a first step to embracing our sexuality. We must also *own* it.

Feeling your sexiness in not only your body, but your mind and spirit as well, will open up your experience in your bedroom, and may also make you feel more beautiful as you walk down the street or more articulate in a dinner conversation. Allowing your sexuality to penetrate your personality and add color to your daily life will enhance the days, and may well bring the power of your whole self into focus. Giving yourself permission to witness and interact with the world through your sexuality is the first step in understanding the connections among our physical, psychological and spiritual selves.

But what does it all mean?

Think for a moment about the answer to this question. What does sex mean to you? We all struggle to define this most basic and integral part of ourselves. The desire to name and define the sexual experience in a general way is the source of much conflict for the individual, the couple and the culture. Thinking of sex as an emergent rather than objective reality is a good place to start. We come to understand our sexuality and its meaning moment by moment, reinventing it each and every time we are sexual.

Our fears around sexuality arise in part from the unpredictable nature of the sex act itself and the intensity of impulses and feelings that have the potential to overwhelm us as much as they do to transform us and our relationships. Sexuality is frightening because each time we move into it, the outcome is never certain, never the same, and the risks never cease. The desire and simultaneous fear of being consumed in its fire is fertile ground for all kinds of addiction and dysfunction.

Our sexual urges are borne in the body and are processed in the right brain, which makes the sexual experience a felt one, more than a cognitive one.[49] In fact, trying to think through it usually cuts off our ability to experience it at all. The mental unpacking of a sexual experience denies its core sensuality, like dissecting the nutritional elements of an extravagant meal.

Defining what constitutes a sexual act in an objective manner is the way we limit our discomfort with the wide range of meaning sexuality embodies. Religious and governmental attempts to restrict sexual behaviors into socially acceptable categories construct artificial standards that simultaneously shame and provoke. The more rigidly we set the boundaries around our sexuality, the more that individuals, and we as a collective, need to repress and silence our sexual selves. The Kinsey data demonstrated that "normal" was a much wider bell curve than anyone would have predicted. Instead of helping us to embrace our sexual selves, the information was repressed for decades.

When we have the courage to let sex educate us about our relationships and ourselves, we are stepping up to one of the most significant levels of freedom and responsibility that this life can offer. Not only does the experience, which is ever changing, hold our attention to the present moment and company completely, but we also automatically move beyond any cultural dictates about our sexuality into an intimate world of our own making. This freedom exacts a cost—not only must we accept the reality and consequences of our own choices, but also we must allow our partner the same freedoms. So much of the dishonesty and judgment about what sex means comes from the inability to be responsible for our own sexuality while allowing our partners the same freedom.

Trust is a basic building block of sexuality. The orgasmic reality of the body taking control can only happen when we are able to fully abandon ourselves to the moment at hand. The trust begins with the belief in yourself. Not having something to prove about your own sexuality leaves room to discover the magic of the mating ritual, as unique as it is universal. Trusting your partner allows the dance of sexuality to play out.

Trust is a basic building block of sexuality.

The most coveted sexual experience on the planet—of ecstatic, transcendent sex—has nothing to do with any socially constructed, objective ideas of sexuality. It is not a spectator sport—and the pornographic images that we buy in great volume are nothing but its shadow. At the root of conception of life itself and all the creativity that lies dormant in us, sexuality is the teacher, the guide, the way to the momentary epiphanies that make us believe in the force of love as the guiding principle in the universe. Real sex can never be bought or sold, only given and received.

Parting Words

Love and work are the cornerstones of our humanness.
— Sigmund Freud

The biggest obstacle most people have to building and sustaining healthy relationships is in themselves. Overcoming our inability to love usually begins in our own hearts. Discovering our own loveliness and believing that we are worthy of the love that begins in us is the ground floor to creating and maintaining loving relationships with others.

It's important to recognize that in relationships, two halves don't always make a whole. A more reliable equation is that one plus one always makes two. Two whole people wholly devoted to the relationship between them provide solid ground for sustainable love.

Overcoming our inability to love usually begins in our own hearts.

I refer often to this quote by Buddha as a reminder to myself: "You can search throughout the entire universe for someone who is more deserving of your love and affection than you are yourself, and that person is not to be found anywhere. You yourself, as much as anybody in the entire universe, deserve your love and affection."

During the three years I devoted to writing this book, I witnessed the end of many relationships. This often made me pause and question my own beliefs in sustainable love. While I recognize that there are some relationships that are better ended, there are many more that never get a fair chance.

Taking the time and making the consistent effort to find what there is to stay for is how sustainable relationships take root and grow. Developing the skills of loving communication; establishing what a promise means; and cultivating loving thoughts are the building blocks for love that works. These practices look different every day. There is no "getting there"—the journey is all we get. When we give up the idea that we could ever have our relationships "figured out" or that we have learned how to love someone, then we are open minded, willing to remain present.

Writing this book has kept me honest about the work of sustainable love in my own family. The work will never end for me in this life; with real love, it is just the color of each day and the way we open up our hearts, heal our wounds and look forward to the next day. Loving is the only choice that makes any sense at all.

L E A R N   M O R E
The Nose Knows

The scent of desire, it turns out, has more to do with our biological

imperative than we might imagine. That magical x-factor in
seeking and connecting to your special someone is actually right
under your nose—or at least in it. Author Rachel Herz's book *The
Scent of Desire*[50] will be the first of many volumes on the often-
overlooked olfactory system that will forever change how we
think about our relationships. And even though I have long been
promoting smell as our primary sexual sense, I had no idea that its
reach went to the very core of the species regeneration.

Our sense of smell and what attracts or repels us is blueprinted
in our immunological gene structure called the MHC, or major
histocompatibility complex. Every individual's own genetic scent
makeup is as unique as his or her fingerprint.[51] What's more, when
it comes to reproduction, the healthiest progeny come from two
individuals whose MHC is most distinct and different from each
other. This assures that any offspring have the widest range of
immune function and therefore are the most disease resistant. This
actually makes perfect sense in terms of our biological imperative
to go forth and multiply, but it also profoundly affects the whole
courting process as well as the likelihood of making your love
sustainable. MHC compatibility is a predictor of not only bearing
healthy offspring, but relationship longevity and inversely the
frequency of infidelity.

Even more remarkable than the biological compatibility of scent between partners is the new recognition that our ability to smell is completely intertwined with our ability to feel.

Recent research on people who suffered anosmia (scent blindness), usually from a traumatic injury to the head, shows that they also became unable to feel a wide range of emotions. The study concludes that "our sense of smell and our emotional experience are fundamentally interconnected, bi-directionally communicative and functionally the same."[52]

"Wake up and smell the roses" is simply good advice. Practice smelling, indulge in scent and taste and bear witness to the emotional response that accompanies this. It will surprise you.

I have been promoting the use of true scent products that enhance your own natural chemistry for years, intuitively knowing that products made with chemicals are not just bad for your most sensitive tissue, but also cover up your own natural odor and may just interfere with our ability to find and smell our true mates. So take this message to heart and as you breathe, inhale deeply. Build your vocabulary and experience of scent especially around the people you love most. It will make you feel better. Cleopatra knew this; she was known to make love on a bed of rose petals ten inches deep.

Love Products

Since the births of my third and fourth children, I had been looking for some kind of product to bring the pleasure back into my intimate experiences. Then almost like a prayer answered, I found a random bottle of love oil on clearance at a small shop in town. With it, I had my first pain-free sex in years. Not only that, but some kind of crazy passion was awakened that I hadn't even known was there. After the bottle was empty, I understood the link between the amazing sex and the love oil. It took months of research and study to figure out how to make it myself, and so the beginnings of Good Clean Love were born.

I turned our guest bathroom into a love oil lab of sorts; that summer my husband and I tested dozens of formulas. That was also the summer that I finally understood: The more I physically loved my guy, the more he turned into the guy I fell in love with. As I spent more and more money on purchasing exotic essential oils and organic oil bases, he never complained. Our lovemaking was better than ever. I was motivated to test out new formulas.

It was summer, and my kids actually still had bedtimes.

Later that summer, while I was picking raspberries, the idea of starting a company to sell love oil came to me. Blending and pouring thousands of bottles by hand seemed simple compared to the Children's Peace Academy that I had been working to launch. Like most great entrepreneurial ideas, the passion (literally in this case) of the need, and the satisfaction of a solution, is enough to keep you learning and going. Origins is the love oil that started it all; it is still the bottle that I reach for each and every time we agree to dive into the mysterious connection of sexuality.

For me now, the scent of Origins is so deeply linked to the feel of my husband's kiss that even when there hasn't been a mood in sight for days, the memories of release and satisfaction that accompany the scent bring me back to the part of me that has nothing to do with all the other hats that I wear all day. Love oil is my ticket to a journey deep inside myself.

I have a cool job, or, as my fifteen-year-old son would correct me, it is "fresh!" I get to imagine and then sell amazing love products. My husband bought into the concept—he gets to be the primary tester. This is a real perk in a love products company. I have learned a lot about product formulation and ingredients over the years, but what I have learned about love and marriage has been even more inspiring.

Love products are an essential part of any good married life and make great reminders on the nightstand. Ever since I started this little love business, our marriage has improved steadily, and our sex life is in a work, amazing.

Good love products should make touching, kissing and smelling each other better.

Good love products should make touching, kissing and smelling each other better. They should be made with natural ingredients that don't leave nasty and sticky residue on your skin. The products you use for love should make you feel like you love yourself (as far as I am concerned, that leaves petrochemicals out of the mix entirely). Surprisingly, more than 90 percent of the over-the-counter lubes available are made with chemicals that were first designed for cars or oven cleaner. Many women have severe reactions to these products; because they are all made with the same base ingredients, many women come to the false conclusion that they don't like them—or they don't like sex. (It's the products...)

When you are young and fit, lubrication is a natural mechanism that just happens, reminding you that you feel sexy. As we age and experience more of life's cycles (kids, nursing, illnesses and some medications), we often don't get those messages from our body. The cool thing, or, well, the "fresh" thing is this: You can apply a good and natural lube to your body and wake up those arousal feelings yourself.

A Quick and Complete Guide to Lubricants

When lubrication is working well, it is invisible, something we don't have to think about. When it isn't working, we know it immediately. An engine without oil locks up in minutes.

A lack of lubrication in intimacy can take on multiple forms and occur for a myriad of reasons. Age, childbearing, nursing, and some medications are often the cause of vaginal dryness and its associated pain in sex. This is not a minor problem. Pain with sex affects 40 percent of women at some point in their lifetimes.[53] Often this physiological issue is accompanied by a lack of sexual drive, because our natural lubrication also signals arousal. I remember in my teens and twenties when vaginal wetness was a fact of life and arousal happened sometimes without my even noticing it. Those body memories are stored deep in our psyche, and the good news is that triggering them can be as easy as finding the right lubrication.

There are many brands of lubricants available on the market. Largely they break down into three main categories: water-based lubricants, silicone-based lubricants and oil-based lubricants. Each category has its benefits and weaknesses, and it is increasingly important to be informed about the choices and consequences associated with different product ingredients. I started my own love products company because so many products that I used after the birth of my third and fourth child only served to further irritate the situation. Soaking myself in late night baths, I often wondered what was wrong with me and why none of these products were helping me enjoy sex. Being exhausted with burning genitals instead of feeling satisfied made it easy to believe that the problem was with me, not the products.

Water-based lubricants are by far the most popular category because they are most often recommended by physicians and are compatible with latex, which many use for birth control. However, because of their ingredient base, which is largely petrochemical, many women experience continuous irritation, burning, and infection with their use. Propylene glycol, a primary derivative used in anti-freeze and brake fluid; polyethylene glycol, an ingredient in most oven cleaners; and methyl and propyl-parabens are very common. The Campaign for Safe Cosmetics, a research arm of the Breast Cancer Fund, has recently identified parabens as potentially carcinogenic and is working to stop their usage in all personal care products. Another popular ingredient in water-based lubricants is vegetable glycerin. There is some debate about glycerin. On the plus side, it is a great anti-bacterial agent and does provide a certain glide, but in large proportions, it has a tendency to inflame yeast problems and usually ends up very sticky and overly sweet.

Silicone-based lubricants are enjoyed by many with great results. Silicone is known for providing smooth and long-lasting glide. Although many lubricant aficionados swear by silicone lube, it is important to take into account the health risks as well as the fact that it does not wash off sensitive tissue with soap and water very easily.

Natural oil-based lubricants offer a sensuous and aromatic choice for individuals who are either allergic to latex or have other birth control methods. Love oils and butters gave me my first really positive and healing sexual experience and inspired me to launch my business in natural love products. The use of olive oil and coconut oil as lubricants is ages old, and for good reason.

I have researched product chemistry and really believe that many intimacy products suffer from a serious lack of imagination. In developing our water-based lubricant, we applied ourselves to finding all natural product ingredients and, thanks to healthy collective questioning and a great lab, we came up with what I would have to say is the best, all natural lubricant available. We create our fragrance and flavor with infusions of whole flowers and herbs. All in all, I really don't think you can get a cleaner, fresher lube. I guarantee it will take twenty years off your sex drive.

Regardless of what lubricant you choose, realize that the body can teach the mind, and arousal and sexual enhancement may be as nearby as the bottle on your nightstand.

The Buzz on Vibrators

By far the biggest category of adult products, after pornography, is toys. The majority—more than 70 percent—are made in China and sold all over the world with a remarkable lack of oversight. A report in 2001 by the Canadian Broadcasting Company (CBC) suggested that the North American market alone is worth $400 to $500 million.[54] These estimates are probably conservative.

While there has been some press on the negative effects of vibrators and the dependence that some women develop on them for finding orgasm, they have also been profoundly instrumental in allowing some women to have an orgasm in the first place.

The range of options available is dizzying. One can find vibrators and like products in every color, size, and material, from soft and squishy silicone to titanium. Even the categories of vibrators and dildos can fill a web page—everything from clitoral, missile, waterproof, erection rings... the lists go on.

With the proliferation of information available online, it is difficult to know even where to begin to find out the answers to even the most basic questions.

There are a few websites that are owned by some friends who always have something to teach me about the range of products and info available. Not only will you find a dazzling array of products, but great information and reviews to help make good choices: Check out: www.goodvibrations.com; www.comeasyouare.com; www.babeland.com; www.smittenkitten.com; www.freddyandeddy.com.

The majority of adult products are made with plastics, which, although this may be stating the obvious, is an important consideration as you become a consumer. Sadly, the lack of regulation and oversight in this industry has created a glut of products that have been found to be extremely dangerous, with both low-quality ingredients and bad plastics which off-gas and leak nasty chemicals.[55] European studies of adult toys have shown extremely high levels of off-gassing of dangerous chemicals such as phthalates in very high concentrations; even at lower levels, these have been linked to cancer and damage to the reproductive system. Being an intelligent and conscious consumer of adult products is an absolute necessity in this unregulated market—so please consider this a health warning and ask about the ingredients.

All of that said, there are some really great eco-friendly and safe toys to use that can add excitement and novelty to the bedroom. As in any industry, you get what you pay for. When I first brought home some cheap phallus-shaped vibrators, my husband was uninspired, to say the least. Be prepared to invest in toys that are responsibly made, luxuriously beautiful, functional and long lasting. Moving up in price moves you from shopping for a vibrator to selecting a pleasure object... a distinction definitely worth the investment.

My favorite companies in the mid- and upper-price ranges include two European manufacturers: The Fun Factory, a German manufacturer of erotic toys at www.funfactory.de and the Swedish manufacturer Lelo: www.lelo.com. Both of these companies offer a wide range of styles and shapes to engage most any couple.

As Einstein said, "Imagination is more important than knowledge." Certainly when it comes to physical intimacy, allowing our imaginations a bit of free reign can only help to unleash some undiscovered passion. I have become a vibrator aficionado, always ready to expand my collection to include more and different sensations.

Shopping and wondering about toys together can be a great appetizer to the main course.

The Story on Sex Books

Joseph Campbell said "I don't believe that anyone knows what sex is. It's the greatest mystery in human life." I think that is the most honest place to start in thinking about books on sexuality. It assumes that we give up our notions of right and wrong about sexual preferences, practices and ideas. It means that we strip away the moral and cultural codes that define sexuality and give ourselves permission to feel normal in whatever ways we move toward our own sexual experiences and expression. Bringing fun and insightful books into your marriage can inspire conversations that build intimacy and provide fuel for the work of keeping your intimacy alive and fresh.

If I were to break these books down into categories, they would include the how-to books, the picture books, the erotic literature, the pornographic books, Tantra books, the unique sex focus books, and the "revitalizing your sex life" books. Popular authors on the topic each have their own unique voice, so finding someone who can speak to you is not that difficult, yet important. Be sure to read a little about the author and his or her qualifications so that you trust the information and point of view that is being shared.

Many of the how-to, picture and pornographic books focus on the physical aspect of sexuality and provide excellent photos and educational content. The DK Series on sexuality is well done and tastefully presented. Some of my other favorite titles in this category include *Sexual Intelligence* by Kim Cattrall; The *Sex Bible* by Susan Crain Bakos; and *Sex—The Whole Picture* by Nicole Beland.

If you are less interested in photos than funny but insightful prose on the topic of oral sex, try the popular books by Ian Kerner: *She Comes First* and *He Comes Next*.

There are many great annual reviews of high-class erotica including *Best Sex Writing*, with new versions every year; *Sweet Life 2—Erotic Fantasies for Couples*; *Best Women's Erotica*; and *Taboo: Forbidden Fantasies for Couples*, the last three edited by the author Violet Blue. She is one of the most well-known and well-read experts in the sex field and writes on everything from cunnilingus to the care and keeping of sex toys.

The brain is the organ that is most neglected when it comes to good sex, and it can completely turn things around when you find yourself in a sexual rut.

There are so many titles on the spiritual side of sex, and many of them refer to the ancient art of Tantra and the yogic spiritual system from which it grew. Browse through the book selection at www.tantra.com. Exploring this deep spiritual side of sex is accomplished in Gina Ogden's latest release on the transformative power of intimacy called *The Heart and Soul of Sex.*

There are also a great number of titles on healing sexual relationships and reigniting the passion in your love life. Because most of us never got more than the cursory labeling of body parts in our sex education classes, these types of books can provide a great basis for understanding the range of "normal" sexual functioning (hint: it is a very wide bell curve). These books also provide helpful tools for dealing with problems that are way more common than most of us realize. One of the best is David Schnarch's recent book *Resurrecting Sex.* Other titles that I recommend include: *Reclaiming Your Sexual Self* by Kathryn Hall; and *The Ten Minute Sexual Solution* by Darcy Luadzers.

Sex books make great gifts for your lover too. Offering a chance to read aloud or share photos of what you each think is sexy is an easy way to get the fire started and laugh together. The *101 Nights of Grrreat Sex* and *The 101 Nights of Grrreat Romance* are actually packaged with each page as a gift to open together. What is important isn't so much the titles that you choose, or that you would even be interested in the same books, but that you build a library of intimacy together. Sharing new and different ideas about what sex means to each of you and what you each need to feel safe to explore is sure to strengthen and enhance your time together.

N O T E S

Additional Resources

Allende, Isabel. *Aphrodite: A Memoir of the Senses.* New York, NY: HarperFamingo, 1998. Print.

Anand, Margot. *The Art of Sexual Ecstasy: The Path of Sacred Sexuality For Western Lovers.* Los Angeles: J.P. Tarcher, 1989. Print.

Angier, Natalie. *Woman: An Intimate Geography.* Boston: Houghton Mifflin, 1999. Print.

Cass, Vivienne. *The Elusive Orgasm: A Woman's Guide to Why She Can't And How She Can Orgasm.* New York: Avalon Group, 2007. Print.

Cattrall, Kim. *Sexual Intelligence.* New York: Bulfinch, 2005. Print.

Chalker, Rebecca. *The Clitoral Truth: The Secret World at Our Fingertips.* New York: Seven Stories, 2000. Print.

Cornog, Martha. *The Big Book of Masturbation: From Angst to Zeal.* San Francisco: Down There, 2003. Print.

Gilbert, Daniel Todd. *Stumbling On Happiness.* New York: Vintage, 2005. Print.

Goldstein, Andrew, and Marianne Brandon. *Reclaiming Desire: Four Keys to Finding Your Lost Libido.* Emmaus, Pa.: Rodale, 2004. Print.

Goleman, Daniel. *Social Intelligence: The New Science of Human Relationships.* New York: Bantam, 2006. Print.

Herbenick, Debby. *Because It Feels Good: A Woman's Guide to Sexual Pleasure and Satisfaction.* [Emmaus, Pa.]: Rodale, 2009. Print.

Herz, Rachel. *The Scent of Desire: Discovering Our Enigmatic Sense of Smell.* New York: William Morrow, 2007. Print.

Kerner, Ian. *She Comes First The Thinking Man's Guide To Pleasuring A Woman.* Harpercollins, 2007. Print.

Lewis, Thomas, Fari Amini, and Richard Lannon. *A General Theory of Love.* New York: Random House, 2000. Print.

Margolis, Jonathan. *O: The Intimate History of the Orgasm.* New York: Grove, 2004. Print.

Moore, Thomas. *The Soul of Sex: Cultivating Life As An Act of Love.* New York: HarperCollins, 1998. Print.

Nelson, Tammy. *Getting the Sex You Want: Shed Your Inhibitions and Reach New Heights of Passion Together.* Beverly, MA: Quiver, 2008. Print.

Ogden, Gina. *The Heart & Soul of Sex: Making the ISIS Connection.* Boston: Trumpeter, 2006. Print.

Ogden, Gina. *Women Who Love Sex: An Inquiry Into the Expanding Spirit of Women's Erotic Experience.* Cambridge, Mass.: Womanspirit, 1999. Print.

Ornish, Dean. *Love & Survival: The Scientific Basis For The Healing Power of Intimacy.* New York: HarperCollins, 1998. Print.

Roffman, Deborah M. *Sex and Sensibility: A Parent's Guide to Talking Sense About Sex.* Cambridge, Mass.: Perseus Pub., 2001. Print.

Schnarch, David Morris. *Passionate Marriage: Love, Sex, and Intimacy in Emotionally Committed Relationships.* New York: H. Holt, 1997. Print.

Schnarch, David Morris. *Resurrecting Sex: Resolving Sexual Problems and Rejuvenating Your Relationship.* New York: HarperCollins, 2002. Print.

Solot, Dorian, and Marshall Miller. *I [heart] Female Orgasm: An Extraordinary Orgasm Guide.* Cambridge, Mass.: Da Capo, Life Long [], a Member of the Perseus Group, 2007. Print.

Wade, Jenny. *Transcendent Sex: When Lovemaking Opens the Veil.* New York: Paraview Pocket, 2004. Print.

Valuable Websites

The Alexander Foundation for Women's Health: www.afwh.org

Go Ask Alice!: www.goaskalice.columbia.edu

Good Clean Love: www.goodcleanlove.com

The Kinsey Institute for Research in Sex, Gender, and Reproduction: www.kinseyinstitute.org

The National Women's Health Network: www.womenshealthnetwork.org

The New View of Women's Sexuality: www.fsd-alert.org

Our Bodies, Ourselves: wwwourbodiesourselves.org

American Association of Sexual Educators, Counselors and Therapists: www.AASECT.org

The Society for the Scientific Study of Sexuality (SSSS): www.sexscience. org

The International Society for the Study of Women's Sexual Health (ISSWSH): www.isswsh.org

Where to Buy: Sex-positive Shopping Experiences

Good Clean Love: www.goodcleanlove.com

Good Vibrations: www.goodvibes.com

Smitten Kitten: www.smittenkitten.com

Come As You Are: www.caya.ca

Babeland: www.babeland.com

Freddy and Eddy: www.freddyandeddy.com

N O T E S

E N D N O T E S

1. "Partners Sculpt Each Other to Achieve Their Ideal Selves: If Successful, Relationship Goes Well." *Science Daily: News & Articles in Science, Health, Environment & Technology.* Northwestern University, 31 Dec. 2009. Web. 08 Aug. 2010. <http://www.sciencedaily.com/releases/2009/12/091216144143.htm>.

2. "Pay It Forward: Elevation Leads to Altruistic Behavior." PhysOrg.com - Science News, Technology, Physics, Nanotechnology, Space Science, Earth Science, Medicine. 3 Feb. 2010. Web. 22 Mar. 2010. <http://www.physorg.com/news184422486.html>.

3. Reach-Out Australia. "Maintaining a Happy Relationship." NSW Family Planning, 28 June 2009. Web. 09 Aug. 2010. <http://au.reachout.com/find/articles/maintaining-a-happy-relationship>.

4. Bahri, Charu. "Intimacy Is Good for Health | Complete Wellbeing." 7 May 2008. Web. 09 Aug. 2010. <http://completewellbeing.com/article/intimacy-is-good-for-health/>.

5. Lewis, Thomas, Fari Amini, and Richard Lannon. *A General Theory of Love.* New York: Vintage, 2001.

6. Barash, David P., and Judith Eve. Lipton. *The Myth of Monogamy: Fidelity and Infidelity in Animals and People.* New York: W. H. Freeman and, 2001. 39.

7. Lewis et al., op cit.

8. "Researchers Find That Middle-Aged Misery Spans the Globe." Welcome to the University of Warwick. University of Warwick, 28 Jan. 2008. Web. 22 Mar. 2010. <http://www2.warwick.ac.uk/newsandevents/pressreleases/researchers_find_that/>.

9. "Menopause, Hormones, The Menstrual Cycle, Hormone Replacement Therapy, Osteoporosis, Estrogen, Progesterone, Natural Therapies." *Alternative Medicine, Complementary Medicine, Integrative Medicine, Mind-Body Medicine, Herbs, Nutrition.* Web. 08 Aug. 2010. <http://www.holisticonline.com/remedies/hrt/hrt_menstr_hormone.htm>.

10. Seligman, Katherine. "Social Isolation a Significant Health Issue - SFGate." Featured Articles from SFGate. San Francisco Gate, 2 Mar. 2009. Web. 22 Mar. 2010. <http://articles.sfgate.com/2009-03-02/entertainment/17212628_1_loneliness-social-isolation-john-cacioppo>.

11. Ibid

12. Belkin, Lisa. "Do You Sleep With Your Spouse? - Motherlode Blog - NYTimes.com." Parenting, Children and Parents - Motherlode Blog - NYTimes.com. New York Times, 15 Sept. 2009. Web. 22 Mar. 2010. <http://parenting.blogs.nytimes.com/2009/09/15/do-you-sleep-with-your-spouse/>.

13. Goleman, Daniel. *Social Intelligence: The New Science of Human Relationships.* New York: Bantam, 2006.

14. Hatfield, Elaine, John T. Cacioppo, and Richard L. Rapson. *Emotional Contagion.* Cambridge [England: Cambridge UP, 1994.

15. Shute, Nancy. "Why Loneliness Is Bad for Your Health." *Health - U.S.News & World Report.* 12 Nov. 2008. Web. 09 Aug. 2010. <http://health.usnews.com/health-news/family-health/brain-and-behavior/articles/2008/11/12/why-loneliness-is-bad-for-your-health.html>.

16. Bliumis, Benjamin. "School Kids, Axe the Social Networking - BusinessWeek." *BusinessWeek - Business News, Stock Market & Financial Advice.* Bloomburg Business Week. Web. 08 Aug. 2010. <http://www.businessweek.com/debateroom/archives/2010/05/school_kids_should_axe_the_social_networking.html>.

17. Martino, Steven C., Rebecca L. Collins, Marc N. Elliot, Amy Strachman, David Eve. Canouse, and Sandra H. Berry. "Exposure to Degrading Versus Nondegrading Music Lyrics and Sexual Behavior Among Youth." *Official Journal of American Pediatrics* 118.2 (2006): 430-41. Official Journal of American Pediatrics, 1 Aug. 2006. Web. 8 Aug. 2010. <http://pediatrics.aappublications. org/cgi/content/abstract/118/2/e430>.

18. Comfort, Alex. *The Joy of Sex.* New York: Crown, 2002.

19. Kerchheimer, Sid. "Sex Better Than Money for Happiness." WebMD - Better Information. Better Health. Web. 22 Mar. 2010. <http://www.webmd.com/a-to-z-guides/features/sex-better-than-money-for-happiness>.

20. Schnarch, David Morris. *Resurrecting Sex: Resolving Sexual Problems and Rejuvenating Your Relationship.* Quill, 2001

21. Ornish, Dean. *Love and Survival: The Scientific Basis For The Healing Power of Intimacy.* New York: HarperPerennial, 1999.

22. Brown, Douglas. *Just Do It: How one Couple turned Off the TV and Turned On Their Sex Lives for 101 Days (No Excuses!).* Three Rivers Press, 2008..

23. Muller, Charla, and Betsy Thorpe. *365 Nights: A Memoir of Intimacy.* Penguin, 2008.

24. "Sex after Marriage. Sexless Marriages. Sexless Marriage." NoMarriage.com - Honest Marriage and Relationship Advice for Men. Web. 22 Mar. 2010. <http://www.nomarriage.com/ articlesexless.html>.

25. Ibid.

26. Passion and Power: The Technology of Orgasm. Dir. Emiko Omori. Perf. Rachel Maines, Dell Williams, Betty Dodson. Wabi Sabi Productions. DVD.

27. Queen, Carol. "It's Masturbation Month! Give Yourself a Hand!" *CarnalNation | Sins of the Flesh.* 1 May 2009. Web. 09 Aug. 2010. <http://carnalnation.com/content/6039/10/its-masturbation-month-give-yourself-hand>.

28. "The Kinsey Institute - Sexuality Information Links - FAQ [Related Resources]." The Kinsey Institute for Research in Sex, Gender, and Reproduction. The Kinsey Institute, 29 Feb. 2009. Web. 22 Mar. 2010. <http://www.kinseyinstitute.org/resources/FAQ.html>.

29. Fenton, Zita. "Masturbation: From Taboo To Doctor's Orders : GoArticles.com." *Article Search Engine Directory: GoArticles. com.* 19 Jan. 2010. Web. 08 Aug. 2010. <http://www.goarticles.com/cgi-bin/showa.cgi?C=2492780>.

30. "What You (and Everyone Else) Are Really Doing in Bed - Redbook." *Sex Tips, Marriage Advice, Getting Pregnant, & Online Sweepstakes - Redbook. RedBook Magazine.* Web. 08 Aug. 2010. <http://www.redbookmag.com/love-sex/advice/what-you-are-ll>.

31. Tepper, Mitch. "Sexual Pleasure: What About Me?" *Sexual Health Network - Credentialed Experts Providing Sexuality Education from Pleasure and Orgasm to Sexually Transmitted Diseases, Sexual Dysfunction, and Sex and Disability.* 4 May 2004. Web. 09 Aug. 2010. <http://www.sexualhealth.com/article/read/love-relationships/keeping-sex-fun/256/>.

32. Charles Moser, in *Journal of Social Work and Human Sexuality* 1988, (7;1, S.43-56)

33. Person, Ethel S. / Terestman, Nettie / Myers, Wayne A. / Goldberg, Eugene L. / Salvadori, Carol: Gender differences in sexual behaviors and fantasies in a college population, 1989, in: Journal of Sex and Marital Therapy, Bd. 15, No. 3, 1989, P. 187–198. See also "What's Really Happening on Campus", *Playboy* October 1976, S. 128-131, 160-164, 169. (see Charles Moser / Eugene E. Levitt: An Exploratory-Descriptive Study of a Sadomasochistically Oriented Sample, in Journal of Sex Research, Vol. 23, 1987, P. 322-337.)

34. Comfort, Alex. *The Joy of Sex.* New York: Crown, 2002.

35. "Men's Health Lists : MensHealth.com." *Men's Health Magazine : Men's Guide to Fitness, Health, Weight Loss, Nutrition, Sex, Style and Guy Wisdom.* Web. 06 Apr. 2010. <http://www.menshealth.com/mhlists/her_sexual_fantasies/index.php>.

36. "Infidelity Statistics." *Lying and Infidelity in Romantic Relationships - Truth About Deception.* Truth About Deception. Web. 10 Aug. 2010. <http://www.truthaboutdeception.com/cheating-and-infidelity/stats-about-infidelity.html>

37. Jamal, Mason. "Men Cheat Down, Women Cheat Up." *BV on Love.* 20 Nov. 2009. Web. 10 Aug. 2010. <http://www.bvonlove.com/2009/11/20/men-cheat-down-women-cheat-up/>.

38. Ciarcia-levy, Joy. "Infidelity: Is Monogamy Just a Myth?" *ABCNews.com - Breaking News, Politics, Online News, World News, Feature Stories, Celebrity Interviews and More - ABC News.* 16 July 2008. Web. 10 Aug. 2010. <http://abcnews.go.com/2020/Stossel/story?id=5380175&page=1>.

39. Friday, Nancy. *My Secret Garden: Women's Sexual Fantasies.* New York: Pocket, 1998.

40. Britt, Robert R. "Love More Powerful than Sex, Study Claims." *LiveScience | Science, Technology, Health & Environmental News.* Journal of Neurophysiology, 31 May 2005. Web. 09 Aug. 2010. <http://www.livescience.com/health/050531_love_sex.html>.

41. Margolis, Jonathan. *O: The Intimate History of the Orgasm.* New York: Grove, 2004.

42. Ibid.

43. Basson, Rosemary. "Women's Sexual Dysfunction: Revised and Expanded Definitions - Basson 172 (10): 1327 -." *Canadian Medical Association Journal - August 9, 2010.* Canadian Medical Association Journal, 10 May 2005. Web. 09 Aug. 2010. <http://www.cmaj.ca/cgi/content/full/172/10/1327>.

44. Brotto, Lori. "How Do You Use Mindfulness To Treat Women's Sexual Arousal Disorders?" *Women's Health and Wellness Information, Tips - EmpowHER.com - Improving Health, Changing Lives.* 12 Sept. 2008. Web. 09 Aug. 2010. <http://www.empowher.com/sex-relationships/content/how-do-you-use-mindfulness-treat-womens-sexual-arousal-disorders-dr-brotto-video>.

45. Weiss, Phillip. "An Orgasm a Day Keeps the Doctor Away ." *Men's Journal*. Men's Journal, 3 Apr. 2009. Web. 09 Aug. 2010. <http://www.mensjournal.com/3-orgasms>.

46. Medvin, Abi. "The Friday Quickie." *TheDartmouth.com | America's Oldest College Newspaper. Founded 1799*. Dartmouth College, 6 Apr. 2007. Web. 09 Aug. 2010. <http://thedartmouth.com/2007/04/06/mirror/the>.

47. Kerner, Ian. *She Comes First: the Thinking Man's Guide to Pleasuring a Woman*. New York: Regan, 2004.

48. Queen, Carol. *Carol. Queen*. Web. 06 Apr. 2010. <http://www.carolqueen.com/pages/bibliography.htm>.

49. Kimura, Doreen. "Understanding the Human Brain." *SFU.ca*. Web. 09 Aug. 2010. <http://www.sfu.ca/~dkimura/articles/britan.htm>.

50. Herz, Rachel. *The Scent of Desire: Discovering Our Enigmatic Sense of Smell*. New York: William Morrow, 2007. Print.

51. Callaway, Ewen. "How Genes Pick Our Mates for Us." *ABCNews.com - Breaking News, Politics, Online News, World News, Feature Stories, Celebrity Interviews and More - ABC News*. 15 Sept. 2008. Web. 08 Aug. 2010. <http://abcnews.go.com/Technology/story?id=5791845&page=1>.

52. Kohl, J. V. *Pheromones.com | The Scent of Eros | By James Kohl*. Web. 06 Apr. 2010. <http://pheromones.com/>.

53. "Low Sex Drive in Women." *MSN Health & Fitness: Health Articles & News – Fitness Tips & Guide*. MayoClinic, 8 Dec. 2009. Web. 08 Aug. 2010. <http://health.msn.com/health-topics/sexual-health/womens-sexual-health/articlepage.aspx?cp-documentid=100186622>.

54. Rosen, David. "The Global Trade in Sex Toys." *CounterPunch: Tells the Facts, Names the Names*. Out of Bounds Magazine, 2 Dec. 2006. Web. 09 Aug. 2010. <http://www.counterpunch.org/rosen12022006.html>.

55. See "Campaign for Safe Cosmetics : Parabens." *Campaign for Safe Cosmetics : Index.* Web. 06 Apr. 2010. http://www. safecosmetics.org/article.php?id=291 and Oppenheim, Leonora. "TV - How To Buy A Green Sex Toy." TreeHugger. 6 Sept. 2006. Web. 06 Apr. 2010. <http://www.treehugger.com/files/2006/09/ treehuggertv_sextoys.php>.

56. "The Kinsey Institute - Sexuality Information Links - FAQ [Related Resources]." The Kinsey Institute for Research in Sex, Gender, and Reproduction. The Kinsey Institute, 29 Feb. 2009. Web. 22 Mar. 2010. <http://www.kinseyinstitute.org/resources/ FAQ.html>.

ABOUT THE AUTHOR

Wendy Strgar is the founder and chairman of Good Clean Love. Her natural and organic product line is endorsed by physicians and sold nationwide. Wendy is a loveologist who writes and lectures on Making Love Sustainable, a green philosophy of relationships that teaches the importance of valuing the renewable resources of loving relationships and family. A sexual health educator, her work is featured at goodcleanlove.com, on her blog at makinglovesustainable.com as well as on Care2.com, Hufington Post.com, NaturalSolutionsmag.com as well as several other green blogs including Intent, Hitched and Green Girls. Married for more than 25 years and a mother of four children, her daily life is the lab for her loveology work. She tackles the challenging issues of sustaining relationships and healthy intimacy with an authentic and disarming style and simple yet innovative advice. Wendy lives in Eugene, Oregon in the beautiful Pacific Northwest.